Out of the Belly of the Whale

Out of the Belly of the Whale

✦

Bridging the gap from sickness to health

Eileen J. Austin

iUniverse, Inc.
New York   Bloomington

Out of the Belly of the Whale
Bridging the gap from sickness to health

The views expressed in this work are solely those of the author and do not necessarily reflect the views of the publisher, and the publisher hereby disclaims any responsibility for them.

iUniverse books may be ordered through booksellers or by contacting:

iUniverse
1663 Liberty Drive
Bloomington, IN 47403
www.iuniverse.com
1-800-Authors (1-800-288-4677)

Because of the dynamic nature of the Internet, any Web addresses or links contained in this book may have changed since publication and may no longer be valid.

ISBN: 978-1-4401-9661-4 (sc)
ISBN: 978-1-4401-9662-1 (ebk)

Printed in the United States of America

iUniverse rev. date: 3/17/2010

Table of Contents

Acknowledgments

Isaac Newton said, "If I have seen more than others, it is only because I have stood on the shoulders of giants." It is because of the legacy of faith that others have left behind that I am able to write and prayerfully entrust this book to guide those who need the 'Master's Healing Touch.'

Jesus said in John 8:32, "You shall know the truth and the truth shall set you free." I seized the opportunity for healing by reading and meditating on inspired books, magazines and tapes. I do not believe you can continue in sickness if you make it a point to saturate yourself with truth from God's word. Napoleon said this about the Bible, "It is not merely a book but a *living thing.*" The key is not to just read the truth but to understand and apply the eternal principles. Then the invisible *Hand of God* can turn the key and unlock the prison door.

I once heard the story of an old woman who was overwhelmed by her circumstances. She went to the local priest for spiritual guidance. The priest listened carefully to her sad tale and then gave her some wise counsel on how to pray.

He suggested, "Fold your hands, bow your head and say whatever comes into your mind." Suddenly the woman began to scream, "Help help!" The startled priest responded, "What on earth is the matter?"

She said, "Nothing but that is the first thing that came into my head."

I suspect God heard and responded to the honest request of that woman because God doesn't stand on formality. You don't have to be in a church sanctuary to connect with your Heavenly Father and get the answers you need. He looks beyond the words to hear the cry of the human heart. Furthermore, people figure out the how and what of praying when they get desperate enough to actually do it!

This book offers more than formulas and get-well schemes because it is an exhortation to embark on your own personal journey to healing and wholeness. Freedom from sickness rests solely in the Divine hand of God Himself but familiar signposts along the way let you know that you are on the right path. I hope this book will be used like a well worn treasure map.

Like the Alaskan gold miners in 1896 who pursued their dream of wealth in the Klondike with every bit of strength and money they could muster, I pursued my dream of health. I am grateful for the many teachers who gave me incite into faith for my healing. By diligently studying the works of great heroes of the faith such as Katherine Marshall, Corrie Ten Boom, T.L. Osborne, Oral Roberts, Benny Hinn, F.F. Bosworth, Wally Quinn, Charles and Francis Hunter, E.W. Kenyon, Kenneth E. Hagin, John Osteen, Doug Jones and Kenneth and Gloria Copeland to name a few, I received insight into my divine healing covenant which was purchased by the blood of my Savior Jesus Christ.

I am especially thankful to my husband Rick, whose patience, devotion and spiritual guidance kept me and the family persevering unto victory. In the midst of an endless health battle, which threatened to overwhelm me, Rick stayed steady, faithful and relentless in prayer. He kept the family trucking along with Jesus, as my Uncle George used to say. I am also indebted to beloved family members like my mom Mrs. Irene Jacobson, sisters, Dr. Leilani Doty and Mrs. Darlene Kelly and my mother in law Mrs. Loena Austin for their prayers, love and support.

I am also indebted to my four beautiful children including the eldest Pete "the Rock," for the many midnight pep talks and courage in prayer, and who refused to give up on having a healthy mom praying with his Godly friends like Dave Rizkowski from ORU.

I am also grateful for "amazing" Grace, for being mom #2, who accompanied me to endless treatments and always found just the right song on the radio especially when dialysis was particularly rough. Our song was, "I Get knocked Down but I Get up Again," remember? How you managed being a senior in a new school while taking care of the other children and running the household is a testimony to your fortitude and strength.

A word of appreciation goes to "jubilant" and wise Joy who spent almost as much time maintaining the household as her older sister Grace. While attending a new school she found time to love me and nurture her younger brother Andy. Her snuggles of encouragement allowed me to persevere through the difficult "dialysis treatment" days.

Finally, to my youngest child, "lovable lion" Andy for the gigantic hugs and caring visits after school. Even though you wanted to rush out and play with friends, you gave time to be with Mom first. Though you were small, you seem to understood when mom was either too weak to go to soccer practice or too weary to get up from bed. A great big hug "right back at you" for faithfully praying and thanking God in prayer each night for healing mom from "no more dialysis treatments" until it finally happened.

Not to be forgotten, Tigger the Cat, who took everything in stride, without losing one wink of sleep or a 1/4 inch off his waistline but who understood and "put up with extra affection and smothering hugs from the children" when days were particularly rough.

A word of thanks to:

Mrs. Mary Onanian, Darlene Kelly for reviewing and editing this book: Mrs. Sylvia Pierce and Dr. & Mrs. Victoria & Mo Unni, Mr. Richard Mangerian, Mr. & Mrs. Humo Mangerian for editing, prayers and encouragement during the writing of the manuscript. Hall of Fame includes Family, Neighbors & Friends who prayed, visited, sent food or expressed encouragement:

Keith, Kahil, and Erin Doty, Lyana Nechyba, Bridget Sherman, Claude & Mildred Branch, Kathy Muni, Ms. Lenore Habeeb, Karen Henderson, Audra& Dennis Bulin, Jill & Skip James, Laura Schaughecy, Georgiana Casela, Mary Abrahamson, Karen & Andy Ritter, Dr. John & Theresa Toney, David & Judy Walker, John & Barbara Stein, Suzanne & Claude Greiner, Gary & Vicky Whiting, Dr. Ricardo & Sara Cervantes, David Fifner, Marianne Fifner, Barbara & Bill Johnson, Jill Hathcoat, Donna Kleinniger, Keith & Leigh Ann Fox, Rick & Marsha Joseph, Dr. Gustavo & Desire Serrano.

Pastor Dale and Kaye Brooks, Dr. Rodney and Adonica Howard-Browne, Pastor Derek and Lorna Howard-Browne, and Pastor Esther and Nick Van Rensburg, Pastor Dick and Roberta Stoddard, Dr. Douglas Wingate, President of Life Christian University.

Chapter 1

More Than a Good Fish Story

○ ○

The word of the Lord came to Jonah the son of Amittai, saying "Arise, go to Nineveh the great city, and cry against it, for their wickedness has come up before Me," but Jonah rose up to flee to Tarshish from the presence of the Lord. So he went down to Joppa, found a ship which was going to Tarshish, paid the fare, and went down into it to go with them to Tarshish from the presence of the Lord.

Jonah 1:1-3

Jonah and the Huge Fish

Winds blew full and steady as the vessel sailed further and further away from the coastal city of Joppa. Salt spray licked the wrinkled face of the old prophet. A flight of birds flew overhead while a calm cobalt blue Mediterranean Sea splashed up small white caps. For now the ship enjoyed a fair wind but storm clouds gathered over the horizon. Jonah never noticed. He was too deep in thought. He had never let God down. That is until now. Being a prophet had never been easy for Jonah but he never envisioned a time when God would give him a job that *he simply could not do*. How could life have become so complicated and difficult? "Difficult, more like impossible," he corrected himself. He had started out top in his class in the prestigious world renown Elisha's School of the Prophets.

Every one of his teachers had prophesied great things because he was the proud son of Amittai. As a young man he was determined to be great like Elijah. In those hopeful days of his youth, he envisioned himself invincible with a future that included anointing kings the stature of Saul and David as his predecessor Samuel the prophet had done.

Once he even dreamed *he was* doing what the prophet Nathan had done. Walking with only a staff in hand, he marched into the splendor of the palace and pointed a bony finger at King David. Confronting the sin and king he declared, "Thou art the man." In his dream, he was the hero, with King David breaking, weeping and repenting on the spot in front of the entire royal court. But romantic imaginations and dreams fled as Jonah faced a reality worse than any nightmare.

Runaway Prophet

"Oh to have been a prophet in the glory days of Israel," Jonah mused. Across the horizon, shadows chased away dreams as dark clouds hid white masses of cumulus clouds.

Jonah shook his old gray head and sighed again,

"How could this have happened to me? Wasn't he a proud son of Amittai of the tribe of Zebulun born in Gath-hepher, with a family lineage tracing back to the possession of land taken with Joshua understudy of Moses," Jonah reminded himself.

It wasn't like he hadn't been a good prophet. Jonah's mind turned over the past years. Weren't his past prophecies responsible for restoring land, leading successful conquests, and enlarging territories? In earlier years and because of him, Israel was actually beginning to return to her former days of splendor...that is before things really started going downhill and the king became disobedient.

Lately all Jonah did was prophesy gloom and doom. It wouldn't have been so bad if the king ignored what he said but must he always do the exact opposite! "A king, more like a spoiled kid," mouthed Jonah. To make matters worse none of his recent prophecies had taken place making Jonah feel small and foolish. Was he loosing his touch? Even the younger prophets looked at him in disdain. No one could possibly understand the pressure that Jonah had been through these last couple of years. Overworked and underpaid. No one appreciated him or his work.

Jonah shook his head in agreement, "Maybe they were right, perhaps, it was time for a younger prophet to take his place." Jonah leaned over the deck railing staring blankly at the whitecaps splashing higher and higher. He was demoralized and his stellar career was finished. Shuddering, he thought about how he could have possibly explained this last word of the Lord to family, friends and coworkers. The idea of quitting had risen slowly in his mind like a full moon on a winter night. When the idea was fully displayed it didn't seem so bad given the impossible job, a hard to please blue blood family and the God of His fathers who wouldn't take no for an answer.

The last speck of land disappeared off the horizon and the peaceful turquoise waters of the Mediterranean were about to show their fury. God was about to lay some heavy correction on a disobedient prophet. After all this was not a divine suggestion from God but a heavenly command!

My Story Begins

Eleven years ago I felt impressed by the Holy Spirit to write a book about a wonderful experience that I had with God during a difficult birthing process with my last child. Many individuals probably would have been encouraged to read about how real God can be to a person in a difficult situation without them having to be super "religious." But being a wife and mother caring for my children including a premature fourth child kept me busy. Certainly too busy to write a book! However, the baby grew to be a healthy child who didn't seem to need me as much, and still I found excuses *not* to write.

God waited patiently. Couldn't He understand how insecure I was about my writing abilities? As more time passed the pressing compassion I once felt for the confused and bewildered people that I had encountered in the hospital while giving birth to my son seem to evaporate like raindrops on hot Florida asphalt. I rationalized there were probably preachers and theologians with better credentials than me who had written lots and lots of self-help books. These books were probably collecting dust on some old church shelf. I reasoned. "Why should I write one more?" If folks really wanted help they could read those already written.

Then I began reading the book of Jonah in the Old Testament. Why had God allowed such a fantastic story to be included? Of course, everyone enjoys a good fish story now and then, but was that what this entire story was about? Certain scholars assert that this type of allegory is often given to point out certain morals that need to be followed. If that was so what could the moral to the story be?

To Jonah the hurting and needy people of a different religion, culture and socio-economic group weren't a priority. 1) He was a prophet not a traveling evangelist. 2) It wasn't in his job description. 3) Furthermore, the city of Nineveh was a long standing city that was an enemy of Israel. So it follows they were also God's enemies! Why would any one want to warn Israel's enemies of impending doom?

Jonah reasoned, "Look Lord, if You want to wipe some dirty gentiles off the face of the planet, *then just do it* and quit bothering me about it!"

Jonah was about to get a refresher course in Ancient Theology 101. **God loves all people, even the so-called wicked ones!**

It was alright if Jonah got in a mess with his sin and cried to God for help, after all he was a prophet and God is *supposed* to help out prophets. That is in God's job description. However, how quickly things changed when God wanted Jonah to help the Ninevites. You see, they just didn't know enough about God to cry out.

The book of Jonah was making more and more sense to me. Suddenly, it became more than a story… I too had justified myself and thought, "I am just a housewife. Are all the unfortunate people in the hospital my problem? Half of them are wicked and deserve to be there!"

This sounded familiar. Maybe Jonah wasn't the only one in need of some adjustments.

Then I felt the Lord say, "Look I wanted you to identify with My point of view not Jonah's." Suddenly, I began to get hot around the collar and squirm in my comfortable arm chair. I was rationalizing disobedience just like Jonah had. "Being busy isn't the same as, well, say being a disobedient prophet or was it?" I went back to my cozy life with my family and being a busy, *busy* wife. I had all but forgotten about those hurting people until something happened that put me in as bad a spot as Jonah had been in and it made me remember.

Chapter Review

1. What message did the prophet Jonah receive from God and what was his response?

    _____

    _____

    _____

Chapter 2

While You Were Sleeping

○ ○

And the Lord hurled a great wind on the sea and there was a great storm on the sea so that the ship was about to break up. Then the sailors became afraid, and every man cried to his god and they threw the cargo which was in the ship into the sea to lighten it for them. But Jonah had gone below into the hold of the ship, lain down, and fallen sound asleep. So the captain approached him and said, "How is it that you are sleeping?" Get up and call on your god. Perhaps your god will be concerned about us so that we will not perish."

Jonah 1:4-6

Divine Intervention

Every good sailor knows the telltale signs of an impending storm and the captain of Jonah's vessel was certainly no exception. He noticed the white playful cumulus clouds rapidly disappearing across the horizon being replaced by ominous black clouds. The flying fish and playful dolphins, omens of good luck, no longer raced carelessly beside the craft but instead they hastened towards some safe and distant ocean. Thus marking an end to spectacular orange sunsets, calm westerly winds and more importantly smooth sailing.

Undisturbed by a dropping temperature, the gray headed captain signaled commands for his sailors to batten down the hatches and prepare for the impending storm. What this experienced crew didn't know was that low pressure and strengthening winds accompanied by the warm waters of Mediterranean would give rise to a dangerous hurricane.

Suddenly the storm hit with all her fury. First, lightening flashed overhead then northern winds began shifting the western bound vessel. Gale winds blew northeast and then southeast threatening to dash the vessel upon the rocks. These swirling circular currents of ocean accompanied by the forceful winds caused the main mast to split in two.

Minutes later the sail shredded hopelessly into ribbons while icy sheets of rain pelted the heads of a frightened crew. They decided there was nothing left to do but to yield, ride the storm out and succumb to the fury of the monster. Far into the black starless night the sailors toiled, praying to their gods until the sun finally arose.

Dawn came giving no relief but instead revealed how truly hopeless their situation was. Meanwhile the wind howled incessantly. One mistake by these weary ancient mariners and the vessel would heave to, roll over and sink. Each man knew that in a storm of this magnitude there would be no survivors. So the men encouraged one another attempting to appease the gods with vacant promises. Perhaps they could return to some nearby coastal port. Unfortunately as the stubborn storm continued, they made little progress.

The tempest had forced them far from any familiar coast. Further and further the violent squall drove them on and still it did not let up. While the ship pitched and rolled helplessly, the captain strained to see through the clouded haze. He knew he needed to keep the vessel far enough away from the craggy coastline lest the vessel smash against the rocks.

Powerless against the storm the sailors tried in vain to heave their precious cargo overboard. But crossed winds and angry waves crashed repeatedly upon the decks pulling the vessel downward into the spiraling sea. When all else failed the crew offered more tearful confessions of sacrifice and rash promises to silent deities about future pilgrimages to unknown hallowed places.

Visions of his precious vessel on the bottom of the ocean floor loomed bleakly before the captain. Requesting 'all hands on deck,' the men continued their vigil to respective deities. The overwhelming sense was that the end was very near.

Only a miracle now could save them.

The scriptures tell us that the crew was so frightened they were praying to whomever they could think of but with repeatedly no positive results. The crew did not know enough to call on one true God of Jonah but God intervened anyway because He had a plan for His disobedient prophet Jonah.

We next see God speaking to them, "Pssst, have you noticed the old guy sleeping in the bottom of your ship?" And notice they did. As the men retrieved the last bale of the flax, they came upon a forgotten old man curled up and sleeping in the hole of the ship. Could he really have been sleeping?

Incensed by this flagrant disregard for their desperate circumstances, the furious sailors dragged the reticent stranger passenger before an already distressed captain. From the captains point of view it must have been outrageous that any one person familiar with their circumstances would not have understood that every hand on deck was necessary as the lengthy struggle had left each mate depleted of every ounce of strength. How could one individual be so disconnected with the world around him and unconcerned about the plight of others? Could anyone be that indifferent about his life, the life of the crew and whether or not they perished? Anyone in their right mind would at least assist in some way, bale water, seeing that his own life was also threatened. Obviously, our captain didn't know much about his passenger. So he asks for a reasonable explanation from Jonah about why he was not at the very least praying.

"What meanest thou, O sleeper, arise call on thy God.
Perhaps, your God will think on us and we will not perish."

Jonah 1:6

The captain had given the ragged old gentleman every benefit of a doubt but now the captain's patience was wearing thin. Upon reflection, and with concern, he decided that their situation was too precarious to anger anyone's deity. Still he wondered about the stranger. Why wasn't he terrified, thoughtful, or was he depressed and simply senile as they truly suspected. After all he did act and dressed eccentric and was very peculiar in his ways. On a good day, the captain could have cared less about the particulars as long as the fares were paid in full but *this was not a good day.*

The captain reasoned that the stranger should at least have enough sensibility regarding their situation. Wasn't Jonah concerned about his life? How about theirs? Up till now Jonah's true identity was still unknown. Certainly no self respecting prophet would purposefully ignore the helpless plight of others. Had he been living in the prophetic cloister colony a little too long? How could he be so aloof and indifferent and asleep in the cargo hole during a raging storm?

It staggers the imagination. We shake our heads in disbelief. How could anyone have such an attitude? Yet, even this was not enough to get our prophet talking so God allowed a more extreme measure to be taken by the sailors that would identify Jonah as the culprit. In the next chapter we will read how God got the morose prophet involved in a game of dice so that he would become a blabber mouth.

My Story Continues

Just when you think you have nothing in common with someone like Jonah your eyes of revelation are opened. It is startling to realize that not only are you similar to Jonah but you could easily write the book and sign your name at the bottom without blinking an eye because in reality *you have become a twenty first century Jonah*.

Jonah is not the only one who falls asleep and lets a desperate humanity fend for itself. Sometimes it is only when you find yourself in difficulty that one even takes notice of others in a dire plight. Many individuals are lost and dying around you every day. My own vessel called life was sailing smoothly along until it came to a screeching halt in September of 1996 when I was diagnosed with kidney failure.

From the very beginning I prayed and believed for a miracle. I knew that God would heal and rescue me. But as the time went on and I was still having treatments, many doubts accompanied me. When God did give me the miracle it was in a way that was humbling. For the rest of my life I would be indebted to the sacrifice of another. In the interim, I became one of those hurting people that God had impressed upon me. This time I would not forget so easily because I was one of them.

My precious sister Leilani after watching me endure two grueling years of suffering and hardship of dialysis treatment stepped forward and willingly offered up one of her kidneys that I might return to enjoy the miracle of good health and be free from my prison of endless and painful treatments. This book is dedicated to her and other family members who gave of themselves so generously on numerous occasions during those two long years of kidney failure and treatments.

What the dialysis treatments did for me was to rekindle compassion for other poor souls that suffer and endure similar treatments and do so without faith, or hope and even with no end in sight to their misery. To me it is unthinkable to endure such suffering and yet still have no faith. How do they endure and make sense of any of this without God? I would like to remind the reader that although I too had innumerable days that were intensely painful and frustrating, but I could go on because of a personal relationship with Jesus Christ.

The health challenges gave me the opportunity for unprecedented growth in my faith and knowledge of Jesus Christ my Savior. This book is about those lessons I learned when days were good and the understanding that came to me during those tearful days of pain and difficulty. I cannot stress this enough. Because of faith in God I was able to endure the day, hours and minutes. I was never alone without the wonderful and loving presence of an Almighty God.

In one sense I would not wish this ordeal on my worst enemy and yet in another way I should be envied because it was a time where like old Jonah in the Bible, I got to experience a revelation of God's grace and mercy heretofore unknown to me. My faith as never before became so precious to me that it was like a jewel of immeasurable worth.

The Bible refers to this as the pearl of great price. It became more important than the air I breathed. I hid *this* pearl called faith in the deepest part of my heart. It was my treasure. Faith got up every morning and faith kept watch over me through what seemed the endless nights.

Behind this faith was God always there to listen through my tears, sorrow, misery and then gave me strength for today and hope for tomorrow. In the end, when the answer to prayer came, I was delivered so completely that I am still overwhelmed by the constant mercy and boundless grace that kept me sane, happy and alive to tell this unique story.

> *You will not be afraid of the terror by night, Or of the arrow that flies by day; Of the pestilence that stalks in darkness, Or of the destruction that lays waste at noon A thousand may fall at your side, and ten thousand at your right hand; But it shall not approach you. You will only look on with your eyes, and see the recompense of the wicked. For you have made the Lord, my refuge, Even the most high your dwelling place. No evil will befall you, nor will any plague come near your tent. For He will give His angels charge concerning you, to guard you in all your ways. They will bear you up in their hands, lest you strike your foot against a stone. You will tread on the lion and the cobra, the young lion and the serpent you will trample down.*

Psalm 91:5-13

This book is not about religion but about *a relationship with an approachable God.* A God who loves and cares for you more than you could ever think or imagine. It chronicles my experiences with God whose entire being is filled with love, mercy and compassion for the individual.

Even if an individual thinks that they are beyond the reach of God. They are not! In fact they are the very ones Jesus came to save. That relationship with God is the most precious knowledge that came out of my experiences. It is this more than anything else that I want to share with you that you too may experience how real God can be during the most difficult trial of your life.

Cory Ten Boom has written the book, *The Hiding Place*. It is the story of a Dutch family who hid Jews in Holland during World War II. It recounts the sad and inspiring tale of this heroic family and particularly the fate of two sisters, Corrie and Betsy Ten Boom. Corrie and Betsy end up at Ravensbruck a horrible concentration camp in World War II Germany. Before Betsy died in the concentration camp she whispered the most amazing words to her younger sister Corrie.

> "… (Corrie, you) must tell people what we have learned here. We must tell them that there is no pit so deep that He (Jesus) is not deeper still. They will listen to us, Corrie, because we have been here."

Like those two precious sisters, Cory and Betsy, I was reminded of something wonderful that God put in my heart so long ago before all the craziness began.

> *I will live and not die and declare the works of God.*

> Psalm 118:17

Like Miss ten Boom not only did I live, but I felt impressed to write about my own experiences so that others might be encouraged and learn how to draw strength from God in the midst of their own storms. You are now holding that book in your hands. During the two difficult years of treatments and various surgeries, the compassion and love of God became seared into my being for others in similar circumstances. Like Cory I hope these next chapters bless you!

> *Then I will give you shepherds after My own heart, who will feed you on knowledge and understanding.*

> Jeremiah 3:15

Chapter Review

1. What does Cory learn from her experiences in Ravensbruck about God?

    _____
    _____
    _____

Chapter 3

The Die is Cast - Jonah's Lot

○ ○

And each man said to his mate, "Come let us cast lots so we may learn on whose account this calamity has struck us." So they cast lots and the lot fell to Jonah. Then they said to him, "Tell us, now! What is your occupation? And where do you come from. What is your country? From what people do you come from?" And he said to them, "I am a Hebrew and I fear the Lord God of heaven who made the sea and dry land." Then the men became frightened and they said to him, "How could you do this?" For they knew that he was fleeing from the presence of the Lord, because he told them

Jonah 1:7-10

Anything but a Blabber Mouth

At this point in the story, Jonah has not volunteered much information even though the crew had brought him before the ship's captain. Perhaps Jonah didn't understand that the hand of God *was* set on exposing him so that he and the crew could be saved. The next event forces Jonah to see *crystal clear*. The forceful hand of Providence moves to get our prophet talking. God's suggestion to the desperate crew is necessary to save their lives.

God whispers a suggestion that they investigate Jonah. "Talk to the man you found hiding in the ship's hole and you will find the answer."

It is apparent based on the outcome of the sailor's predetermined conclusion was that whomever the lot fell to, was the individual who would be blamed for their present disastrous circumstances. Drawing lots, Jonah probably hanging on to the sides of the ship, draws the short end of the stick. The crew asks the mysterious foreigner some pointed questions. Sadly, then and only then is the true identity of the prophet revealed.

Drawing lots to determine the winner or culprit in this case, was as common a practice in ancient times as throwing a die or flipping a coin is today. But it is still an uncomfortable revelation when we realize what the lengths God had to go to so this card carrying preacher would 'fess up' and talk to the heathen sailors. No mere hurricane was enough for Jonah. He never volunteered one more word than was necessary to the sailors until they ask him point blank. He had the truth they needed to save their lives and yet not one word about his job description or mission or even belief until they drew lots and shook it out of him. We feel the crew's frustration as we scratch our head perplexed. "How could you do this?" For they knew he was fleeing from the presence of the Lord, because he told them. How could Jonah be so detached?

No reasonable explanation for his lapse is plausible; we only know that when the lot fell to Jonah his memory loss was over. He decided to, in modern vernacular; *go on the 'Oprah Show' to tell all.* After the revealing his credentials and mission to the crew, they are first perplexed, shocked and finally alarmed.

It is a fearsome thing to fall into the hands of the living God.

Hebrews 10:11

Even heathens and the non-churched understand that it is a fool mission to try and run from God. How is it that people with no religion are quicker to see what is **not** obvious to those of us who are churched? Certainly a vessel pitching and rolling violently, on the verge of sinking would do the trick. Apparently not! It is not enough that our prophet will stand before God and give an account for his actions but we ask ourselves why should the innocent suffer for one of God's disobedient servants?

Sometimes we look at our twenty-first sophisticated technology century and say, "My how things have changed." Then, we read a story like this and are confronted with the facts regarding the character weaknesses of people and realize, "Maybe things really haven't changed that much." The innocent still suffer for the actions of the guilty. In this case, the guilty was a so-called, God fearing man!

The Phoenician sailors had asked Jonah what my nephew Erin would call the "*$64,000, Cotton Eyed Joe*" question. Where do you come from, where do you go, who are your people and what do you know?

Then they said to him, "Tell us, now! On whose account has this calamity struck us? What is your occupation? And where do you come from. What is your country? From what people do you come from?"

Jonah 1:8

On the surface these appear to be simple questions. If so then why doesn't Jonah answer them? Could it be that he was beginning to be remorseful or perhaps really nervous? According to scripture, these are the two answers given.

And he said to them, "I am a Hebrew and I fear the Lord God of heaven in the true God who made the sea and dry land."

Jonah 1:9

Essentially he said, "Look fellas, my God is the true God who made everything including the heaven, earth, and even you!" Although verse nine does not say or mention that he told them about his job description or even his occupation we do know that he must have given them more information than what is recorded in the text because by verse ten the sailors had this to say.

The men knew that he was fleeing from the presence of the Lord, because he had told them!

Jonah 1:10

What we can conclude is that even though scripture has not recorded all the details that based on the response of the men in Jonah 1:10, we can surmise that Jonah indeed had preached to them. Often in scripture, the reader must read and think between the lines remembering that this was not a history annul that records each detail but a story where the moral takes preeminence.

As I prayed about this dilemma it began to dawn on me that Jonah was not inclined to be a verbose Shakespearean writer only a simple Hebrew prophet. As such, Jonah was expected to record important events for posterity. At the very least, Jonah should say enough to keep him from experiencing, Whale Belly II, the Sequel. The point wasn't, would anyone *believe* that a huge fish had swallowed Jonah and carried him to his destiny to preach to the enemies of Israel? From his point of view, the important thing was that he *had* a whale of a story to *tell* the friends back home.

One can prayerfully draw their own conclusion based on the personality of the main character revealed from scripture. That he probably was equally as long winded to the sailors, given the chapter two discourse.

However, it would not surprise me if *in fact* Jonah was longwinded like most preachers! He probably went on and on and talked their ears off but only records the event's particulars enough for the reader to know what transpired. I suppose we can't blame him, after all no one likes to embellish the part where God exposes your dirty laundry.

Those of us who have children understand this. A parent asks their children, how the school day went and the child replies, "Fine." Does the parent have the smallest notion of what transpired in that eight hour day? Yet if something noteworthy happens such as my daughter talking to the latest dreamboat at school or my son catching the winning tackle at recess then we hear and hear about it endlessly. I guess it is human nature. We don't give a detailed account of anything unless we are center stage.

So it was with Jonah, when he finally got to record his story, he included a brief summary of the conversation that he had with the ship's crew. We know that by verse ten, he told them who he was, what his mission was about and why he was on their boat.

And that dear friend is why they were terrified.

Edge of the Precipice

Angie Presod had worked hard all afternoon on the painted tri-colored creation of the Olympic ringed banner. "Eileen," she hollered at me from the garage, "We've got to have just the right symbol!" She proudly held up the newsprint for me to see and queried.

"Do you think it captures the victorious spirit of the moment?" Angie read the banner half out loud and half to herself. "Teach the Dream- Happy Tenure Rick."

"Are all the colors bright enough?" she asked looking over her shoulder at me.

"Definitely," I said, looking at the vivid red, green and gold masterpiece. Secretly, I thought the banner frivolous, but now I had to agree with Angie as she wiped her sweated brow that it did set a victorious mood for the party. We were celebrating my husband Rick's 'gold medal' accomplishment called tenure.

As a college professor, tenure at a university meant not only the new title of 'associate professor' but also was an acknowledgement by peers of scholarly and professional achievements and the opportunity to stay there until retirement. The Saturday evening party seemed to fly by as we joked, laughed, ate, talked and ate some more. Our hard working physician friend, Dr. Jim Etheridge had written down the name of a particular nephrologist in Tampa so I could get my blood work checked and blood pressure refilled. Before we knew it, the evening was over and my husband and I were at the front door, hugging the necks of our friends and saying goodbye.

Everyone agreed it had been a wonderful party. Even my sometimes hard to please older sister, Leilani had offered, "Just like old times when we were kids at grandma's!" Our Armenian ethnic roots insisted that each guest be stuffed with food and loved like they were family. We certainly felt blessed to have such good friends. In the days and weeks ahead I would learn how precious these and other friendships were to me and especially my sister. Could we ever begin to imagine the incredible struggle we were about to embark on?

The house seemed quiet and peaceful as I loaded the last of the glassware in the dishwasher. Rick and I moved into the family room putting our feet up on the coffee table as we proceeded to sip two cold glasses of iced tea. Breathing a sigh of relief we gazed around the furnishings of our beautiful new home.

Life appeared to be secure, predictable and stable. Rick got up from the couch and began to pull down the huge newsprint sign from over the fireplace. He folded it carefully and then sat down again beside me, picking up the tea mug. Our hearts were content and full. Our three children Pete, 18, Joy, 13 and Andy, 8 slept peacefully. Grace, 16 our fourth child was in Hong Kong on a missions trip with Teen Mania but she had remembered to call her father and congratulate him.

Like knights of old we relished our victory and daydreamed about our next conquest and dragon to slay. College money for the children! My eldest son's future appeared bright but expensive. Although Peter had earned a partial academic scholarship to Oral Roberts University it still seemed costly. He eagerly looked forward to be an entering freshman in the fall.

How could we have ever imagined that the same life's journey that had provided us with such an exuberant mountaintop experience would similarly plummet us to the valley below? Still, we rolled blissfully along heading straight towards the cliff. An enormous and dangerous precipice loomed in the shadows.

God in his mercy had prepared us. He had made sure that our seatbelts were fastened. With Him always as the extra passenger we were more than ready to face this challenge.

> *"Many are the afflictions of the righteous but the Lord delivers us out of them all."*

Psalms 34:19

God doesn't keep us from the difficulty He simply delivers us despite them. This is the wonderful and amazing truth of the gospel. In the months that lay ahead I could identify with the helpless feelings of those unprepared Titanic passengers that drifted helplessly towards destruction. Unlike those responsible for the safety of that vessel, God saw to it that the life boats were prepared. Although you may feel unprepared to face challenges and tests around the corner but with God's help you will succeed.

Tigger, our stripped tabby cat meowed noisily at the back door as Rick and I quietly sipped on our tea, demanding attention and some delicious dinner scraps and we snapped back into reality.

A hot Indian summer of September 1996 was flying by. We had taken Pete to Oklahoma and, although he "said" he missed us a great deal, he was in reality happily settling into his new campus life at Oral Roberts University. I was my missing one of my *baby* chicks even though he was over 6'2 1/2 inches and 210 lbs!

Fortunately for us, on the home front, our eldest daughter Grace, a senior at Gaither High School had returned back from an exciting mission's trip to Hong Kong. She kept us occupied with many wonderful stories while adjusting to a busy and challenging academic school year. She would soon need all of her newly acquired faith skills on the home front.

Joy, always a wee bit shy was facing lots of middle school challenges. She had managed to meet another equally shy friend Brian who just happened to be a pastor's son from a church called 'Victorious Life.' They got better acquainted while they waited for their 'late' moms after school each day.

Our youngest son Andy was busy mastering his goalie position in the neighborhood roller blade matches that were held daily after school with friends Matt, Tyler and Chase.

Our whirlwind and happy lifestyle was about to come to a screeching halt. Fortunately God, as only He can do, had prepared us. His unseen hand moved quietly behind the scenes positioning people around us like a pro strategizing pieces on the chess board. Our family sailed unknowingly upon a tranquil sea heading straight for the greatest squall that our peaceful family had ever experienced. We only reason we never sank was because God was with us and in us. We experienced Him as 'peace' in the midst of a storm.

I was proud of myself and hoped that no one could have guessed that I was in my mid forties. I was fanatical about controlling my weight, swam more than a half a mile three times a week, neither drank alcohol nor smoked. Teaching part time at the local university and overseeing teaching interns kept me busy. At home I was chief bottle washer, chauffeur, and soccer mom.

In the back of my mind, one thought nagged in my mind.

"Take out the dog eared paper on the bureau with the name of the nephrologist from Jim and make that appointment you keep putting off to check out the blood pressure medicine."

So I did. In Jim's scrawled physician's hand writing I deciphered the nephrologist's name and phone number and made the appointment.

Rick and I went together to the appointment on a Friday. The exam appeared uneventful except my blood pressure was high. Dr. Alveranga wanted some routine blood work drawn along with some urine samples. Monday morning rolled around and was hectic as usual. I got the kids off to school including dropping off Joy, jogged a little bit and even swam my usual half a mile. The day rushed by with errands and laundry and before I knew it, I was racing back to pick up Joy.

Returning home, I walked into the house and noticed that Grace had an uncomfortable look on her face. There had been an urgent call from the nephrologist, Dr. Alveranga, regarding the test results and I was to call back immediately. Suddenly the phone rang and it was Dr. Alveranga. As I picked the phone up I heard the words that would radically alter the course of my life.

Dr. Alveranga began by saying that she hated to tell me this on the phone but the tests revealed that I was in kidney failure. She went on to say that I had one of the worst test results that she had ever seen. I almost dropped the phone. In truth, she was astonished that I was even able to walk around. Suddenly, my knees began to buckle. As the blood drained slowly from my face as I found a kitchen seat.

Intuitively, I reached for Grace, standing by and though she didn't understand what was happening knew that she needed to be right there. With a frightened and confused look on her face, she let me grip her hand tightly.

"Furthermore, your schedule must be cleared immediately and you are to report to the hospital the next morning at five for a surgery so an access for dialysis can be put in your neck. You must have treatments this week or..."

No, explanation was needed for what the 'or' meant. I knew my life was in danger I recounted that inner voice that kept urging and tugging at me to have my blood pressure checked by a doctor. In reality *that* had been the voice of God. Through a "coincidence" of timing my life was spared.

"Are you O.K. Mrs. Austin?" Dr Alveranga had asked. "Yes," I lied. In truth I was terrified as I slowly put down the receiver. She closed by adding that if I hadn't gone this past Friday I might not have made it to the end of the week.

Grace held my hand. Oh, the precious comfort that girl gave me that day. One look at my face and she knew something was dreadfully wrong. As we sat there quietly, my throat seemed to close up, unable to get those words out. It was surreal as if the entire world stopped. She waited patiently until I managed to find my voice and say the words so horrible; it simply makes my blood run cold just thinking about it.

Folks say that sometimes hearing the diagnosis is worse than the disease itself. There is a lot of truth in that. If you can survive the evil report and pick yourself up from that then you will probably live to tell the end of the story. President Roosevelt said it best, "We have nothing to fear but fear itself."

Then again, fear is a formidable adversary.

I informed my two girls Grace and Joy with strength that still amazes me. I even managed to attend my son's P.T.A. meeting that evening. I must have looked a sight for my next door neighbor Butch Bell walked across the room because he was so concerned about how I was. I blurted out the evil diagnosis as best as I could while trying to stay composed. With a startled look, he asked what he and his wife Janet could do.

Mechanically, I said, "Pray."

Prayers meant everything to me. When a fear of enormous magnitude attempted to engulf me and gripped my heart, I noticed that something amazing would always happen. A peace of equal, no I must say greater than that fear countered it. This peaceful power engulfed me and at that precise moment a scripture rose up within me. Oh, the wonderful power of prayerful saints.

> *The terrors of death have surrounded me, and horror hath overwhelmed me.*
>
> Psalms 55:5 & 6

David, the King of Israel had written this verse almost 2,000 years ago, but instantly I understood his feelings. I recounted how God had been trying to get my attention that some evil plan was in the works. Earlier in the summer I had a nightmare that was so intense, that when I awoke, I called two prayer warrior friends Audra Bulin and Beth James to immediately pray for me. A premonition is what it is sometimes called when an individual senses that something horrific is about to transpire, although the specifics may be quite obscure.

The Bible says that there is an enemy of our soul and his name is the devil. This fiend survives and thrives on our fears just as God works though our faith. He worked hard on me that day for I could feel his icy hands about my neck, pressing my jugular and whispering in my ear, "The good life, as you know it is over."

Unfortunately, this would not be the last time I would hear that sinister voice speak words to my emotions and mind so I quickly learned strategiesthat would defeat him.

Years ago when I was young, I remember my brother Peter was enamored with the Civil War and the military strategies of armies long past. Unfortunately, one day my 19 year old brother marched off to the real war in the 1960's never to return. Perhaps that is why as I grew older, I had a fascination for Civil War memorabilia and places like Gettysburg, Bull Run and Vicksburg. When traveling my husband and I would make a point to visit a battlefield especially if we were traveling close by. The breezes whispered to remind me of a different day of untold suffering and mangled young men's bodies. Looking at those daisy covered meadows and green lush fields it was difficult to remember those tempestuous battlefields once were covered with the crimson blood of young soldiers. Now, I too was in a battle and needed strategies that would defeat this invisible foe. To presume upon victory with such a formidable enemy was a fatal tactic that many an enemy has used to successfully deceive and defeat a young and inexperienced soldier. How many northern and southern soldiers had gained a victory on a given day but fell in battle never to live and tell about the victory they purchased with their own blood. Would I be one of life's casualties as my brother had been? I prepared myself for battle with this promise from scripture that to this day still holds dear to me.

> *I shall not die, but live, and tell of the works of the Lord. The Lord has disciplined me severely. But He has not given me over to death.*

Psalm 118:17

A Weapon called Safety Harbor

The Bible and the Holy Spirit are two of the greatest weapons that God has given us to defeat an enemy. We also have someone who will always be with us. His name is Jesus. Unlike a human friend or brother, He cannot be lost. And I began to realize that when a report from a doctor would create an overwhelming fear in my mind. If I began to pray out loud or quietly within myself, a peace countering the fear would arise seemingly from the depths of my soul and vaporize the fear.

This quiet strength from some secret Source began to grow like the distant light of a faithful lighthouse. Later I learned that this was the work of the Holy Spirit of God that resided within every person who names the name of Christ. Flashing hope, the Holy Spirit within you even under tremendous pressure will begin to buoy you up. He then positions you to face hope like a vessel moving towards a glowing beacon of light through the night's thickest fog. His job is to light the vessel's path, guiding it safely away from the craggy rocks through the fog until it reaches the harbor safely.

In the two years on dialysis I never missed work due to sickness except in the first weeks when I was hospitalized. To my colleague's amazement, not only did I return to work within weeks but I finished the semester never telling my students or other individuals the extent of the sickness. I refused to dwell on it and *act sick*. Because God was at work, inner strength was accessible, and my soul was at peace.

That same evening I called my pastor Dale Brooks. He wasn't home but his wife, Kay was. She said that she would put me on the church prayer chain and have the pastor get in touch with me as soon as it was possible. When my husband arrived home that night I got his supper and then had him sit down to tell him the incredible news. We talked and prayed together as a family, just as we have always done. Rick then called Pete in Tulsa, Oklahoma. Pete wanted to come home to help the family but Rick had this to say to our oldest son.

"No. You are in the best place in the world for prayer. What your mom really needs now is prayer and lots of it. Go up to the Oral Roberts Prayer Tower where those praying hands are and pray! If there is one place on earth where the folks know how to pray and touch God, Oral Roberts is that place!"

And that is exactly what our son did. Furthermore, he got his friends Chris, Dave, Geno and Mike on his dormitory wing to pray and fast along with all of his Godly professors. Meanwhile Grace called her friends at "Teen Mania." After two missionary trips, she had gotten to know their staff pretty well, so they and their families prayed.

I was also placed on many prayer chains around the world in the days, weeks, and even years that followed. I believe it is because of those prayers that I am alive, strong and healthy today. As Shakespeare aptly put it, "We are rich in our friends."

God in His great wisdom had orchestrated and positioned not only our family but our friends and extended family in such a way that prayer warriors were poised and ready for battle. Thank God! The outpouring of love and support that we received was beyond our wildest dreams and these folks stayed and supported us through an ordeal that would last for two long years!

As I now look back over my experience I can only say that surely the unseen hand of God Himself kept me steady. Rick and I have always been fans of the Sherlock Holmes mysteries. There is a famous line from *The Hound of the Baskervilles* where Sherlock turns to a young lady, who has been almost the victim of a murderer's sinister plan and says,

"I think that on the whole you have had a fortunate escape. You have been walking for some months very near to the edge of the precipice."

To that I can only add a hearty, *"Amen."*

Chapter Review

1. Name some of the weapons that God has given us to defeat our enemy, Satan?

    _____

    _____

    _____

Chapter 4

Rebel with a Cause

o o o o o o o o o o o o o o o o o o o o o o o o o o o o o o o

So they said to him, "What should we do that the sea may
be calm for us?"— for the sea was becoming increasingly
stormy. And he said to them, "Pick me up and throw me
into the sea. Then the sea will become calm for you, for I
know that on account of me this great storm has come upon
you." However, the men rowed desperately to return to land
but they could not, for the sea was becoming even stormier
against them. Then they called on the Lord and said, "We
earnestly pray, O Lord, do not let us perish on account of
this man's life and do not put innocent blood on us; for
Thou, O Lord, hast done as Thou pleased."

Jonah 1: 11-13

What Should We Do

What did the Prophet Jonah reveal to these hardened sailors that had them
shaking and quaking in their sandals?" And why should they try to rescue
the very one who earlier they had accusingly dragged before their captain?
Each time I finished with one set of questions on Jonah, it seems as though
another armada of new ones came sailing over the horizon of my mind, *pardon
the pun*. For example:

Was Jonah *really* as rebellious as everyone makes him out to be?

If he was, then why was God busy chasing him? Why drag this thing
with Jonah out?

Couldn't God have ended all the drama by just letting the vessel sink?

If God had asked for an opinion on the situation, most of us would have sent Jonah and the wayward crew to the bottom of the ocean floor and quickly! End of story! But God was being patient with this man and the crew because he had a different ending in mind. Deciding to look closer, I took out my Sherlock Holmes magnifying glass, metaphorically speaking and did some research on the prophet's background. When I did, this Old Testament Book opened up like oysters on the half shell.

We know that Jonah was one of the Old Testament's Minor Prophets. Scripture records that in II Kings 14:25, Jonah, this son of Amittai was born at Gath-hepher. This information is given so the reader understands that the author had an impressive pedigree and had the *right* to express his views on the political world. Jonah's family tree traced 'their roots' all the way back to the time of Joshua or the founding of Israel! That would be like comparing Jonah's family to an American that traced their roots to the Pilgrim Fathers and the Mayflower sailing in 1620.

Jonah was also responsible for restoring the coastline of Israel 'from Hamath unto the sea of the plain, according to the word of the Lord God of Israel.' Some scholars suggest that this Gath-Hepher, a tiny village referred to as El-Messhed was several miles north of Nazareth. In other words he helped to enlarge the borders of Israel.

As we think about a timeline for this prophet, he probably ministered from 780-750 B.C. or about eight centuries before Christ. This means that he was privileged to live in the days of some of Israel's greatest prophets, Elijah and Elisha.

In earlier years, King David's reign had brought conquest of surrounding lands and unity to Israel while his son King Solomon had brought peace and unprecedented prosperity. However, by the time David's grandson Jeroboam ruled, ten of the tribes had seceded forming the northern kingdom of Israel, while the southern kingdom renamed itself Judah.

Then there was a succession of four kings Nadab, Baasha, Elah, and Zimri. With them, Israel's influence and unity waned and unraveled as the leadership drifted further from their Godly roots and heritage. Meanwhile, in the Northern Kingdom, during the depraved dynasty of Omri, things really eroded from bad to worse.

Omri's son called Ahab intensified the nation's problems, by marrying a beautiful Phoenician princess who later became the infamous Queen Jezebel. Under their wicked rule, Jonah would most likely have been considered one of the "sons of the prophets" who trained for ministry under the prophetic anointing of Elijah and Elisha. Imagine living during these tumultuous times!

Jonah's Spiritual Roots

To understand Jonah background, we must take a look at the prophets Elijah and Elisha. What did they do to incur the wrath of the royals? And how did they create a spiritual influence that impacted Jonah's world?

We must also remember that God has always had a world vision. God used these two great prophets to create a significant backdrop for Jonah's world, by staging events that included many players in both the religious and secular arena. All Jewish and Christian scholars know and reference events in the lives of these great men that lived nearly twenty-seven centuries ago. That in itself should merit great respect as they laid the foundation stone because Elijah mentored Elisha, who in turn mentored Jonah.

As a 'Son of the Prophets, 'young Jonah trained for his prophetic ministry much as a seminarian today would attend a Bible College under Elijah and Elisha who were considered 'Fathers' to the young men. Furthermore, as if to secure the prominence in God's annals, Elijah is reintroduced into future world events, centuries later, by appearing with Jesus Christ on the Mount of Transfiguration in Matthew 17:2.

Understanding this background information reveals the prominence that Jonah enjoyed during his entrance into Jewish history. Although his story records only four meager chapters in the Bible, he was by no means insignificant to his times.

Jonah and his colleagues the prophets lived and worked during a critical time in Israel's history. The effectiveness of a prophet's ministry determined whether or not Jews would continue to worship the one true God and enjoy blessings as such. The destiny of the nation rested upon the resolve and determination of her prophets who would either turn the nation back to God or see its demise and defeat under the ruthless tyranny of surrounding warlike nations including Egypt, Philistia, Phoenicia, Syria, Assyria, and Babylonia.

Never had so many been dependant on so few.

From a King's view point, it may have been shrewd to make treaties with foreigners but from God's point of view it was compromising because they no longer relied solely upon God.   Also, alliances introduced Israel to heathen practices of the surrounding nations who were ruthless, corrupt and wicked. Some of the practices of worship were detestable, and even included human sacrifice!

Like removing the haze left by a window cleaner, I was finally able to clearly gaze into the book of Jonah. Initially, the book of Jonah represented an enormous jig saw puzzle but now piece after piece was fitting together. By understanding the historical significance of the book, this enigmatic book's relevance became obvious with Jonah's role in the prophetic scheme of things beginning to unfold. Digging into Jonah's spiritual roots meant observing Elijah the Tishbite. As a Hebrew prophet of the 9th century, Elijah grandfatherly influence on Jonah was unparalleled. Elijah formed the foundation stone for the builders of subsequent prophetic ministries like Elisha, Jonah, Obadiah and Amos to name a few. There are no words to relay the wealth of understanding that can be uncovered by studying Elijah. Stumbling across him was like digging and finding the "mother load" vein of prophetic thought which pervaded Jonah's day.

King Ahab's steward, Obadiah had the foresight to observe Elijah's movements first hand and recorded the miraculous particulars and events in the Old Testament book of Obadiah.   It is because of the precise record keeping of this devote believer in God, that we have key information and a wonderful picture of the character of Elijah the prophet. Obadiah insisted that the spirit (or wind) of Yahweh (God) was wont to whisk him (Elijah) away to nobody knows where. (I Kings 18:12). Prophets like Elijah were often held in great reverence and respect by the average individual because of their miracle working power, which served to validate their position and to keep the nation from self destructing.

> *For it came about, when Jezebel destroyed the prophets of the Lord, that Obadiah took a hundred prophets and hid them by fifties in a cave, and provided them with bread and water.*

> I Kings 18:4

The detestable worship of Baal, the fertility god, was introduced from Phoenicia when King Ahab's father Omri encouraged his son to marry the Phoenician Princess who became Queen Jezebel. Jezebel was an example of one of those foreign marriage alliances that God despised. She murdered the prophets of Jehovah replacing them with Baal priests and worship. God needed strong men like Elijah the prophet on the scene to counter these forces. Unfortunately, Elijah's tenacity for God singled him out for unprecedented wrath by the royal household particularly when he stood between Queen Jezebel and her immoral worship of the 'detestable' deity Baal.

Queen Jezebel made being a prophet in the time of Elijah hazardous to one's health. For this reason, we often find these prophetic ministries living semi nomadic lives, emerging only from the desert when absolutely necessary. These arbitrary appearances made them appear disconnected from the mainstream of life and times. Often they had to be or else their lives would be in jeopardy. Unfortunately circumstances prevented Elijah from completely routing out this counterfeit religion. However Elisha, Elijah's successor completed the job. Elisha routed out the last of the Baal worshippers from Israel's Northern Kingdom and temporarily diverted the worshippers of this religion.

Elijah's influence on Jonah was profound. The job description of being a prophet in the Old Testament included something that I will simply refer to as the prophetic stance or "prophetic attitude towards life." This included contempt for the "royals" who were corrupt and splendid in their lifestyle. The prophets also harbored a singular attitude of devotion towards God and a willingness to do whatever it took to rid Israel of her foreign, pagan powers. This meant notably, a crude appearance which starkly contrasted the affluent dress of the day.

By locating some of these ancient places on Bible maps, Jonah the man, and his attitudes about the nations were shaped. Formerly eccentric actions of the prophet were beginning to make sense. He was from a small village of Hath-Kepher, which today would be in the modern city of Nazareth. Looking at the map, we note that to the north lay historic Mt. Carmel, the place where Elijah tested, sacrificed, and ultimately single handedly destroyed the 450 prophets of Baal. Further west towards the coast lays Phoenicia and south of that was a tiny strip of Israel's seaport city of Joppa where Jonah headed for his ocean liner travels.

Immediately south of Joppa was the infamous nation Philistia home of Goliath (I Samuel 17:1-4). By traveling northeast above and beyond Nazareth, lay Syria. To the south of Nazareth was Samaria, high on a mountain this new capitol for Northern kingdom of Israel was what Ahab built for his Queen Jezebel. Further to the east lay Nineveh capitol city of Assyria and to their immediate south lay Babylonia in all her glory with none other than the breathtakingly beautiful capitol city known as Babylon.

By tracing events on a map, we saw that Jonah's world was affected by politics and religion much as our world is affected by the Arab-Israeli crisis. Although kings and armies think that they effect change, we know it is God behind the scenes orchestrating all events. He alters the true course of history while implementing His Divine will. Regardless of appearances, God is the One in charge of the world. This is My Father's world!

While prophets Elijah and Elisha changed the world they lived in, the young impressionable Jonah tenaciously, watched, and anticipated that his time would soon come. Time did pass and the relentless and resolute prophet was tested and poised, ready to take his place in the annals of Israel's history.

As the mythical phoenix rising from ashes past, so Jonah, the man with heaven's destiny, emerged singular from the prophetic masses. Despite protest initially, the eccentric prophet finally carried out God's mission to a cursed and dying world. God has always been concerned about a confused hurting humanity so He lovingly, patiently and repeatedly coached his athlete. If

God had prepared the man Jonah, then why was Jonah so reluctant? Did the man feel equal to the task?

God told Jonah to confront Nineveh. This was no small task. As the capitol of Assyria, Nineveh stood proud and haughty. Located on the eastern bank of the mighty Tigris River, it was one of the greatest cities of the ancient world. A complex city that would rival New York City, it boasted splendid temples and palaces. One of the royal palaces had 71 rooms with walls lined with sculptured slabs and possibly carved ivory walls. Its library alone housed more than 22,000 clay slabs.

When unearthed within its actual walled city Nineveh was nearly three miles in length and one-half a mile in breadth just as the scripture verifies.

God had positioned the players, set the stage and drawn the curtain. Jonah had been selected to make his debut as the leading male actor in his day. The scene began. God, the director, was ready to let the cameras roll. Today was the day, Nineveh was the place and this was the hour. Jonah emerged on the world scene to take his place in God's Hall of Fame. This is what he had lived for and if necessary would die for.

The prophet was to go and present the inhabitants with an unusual message, "Repent or be destroyed by God." This was no empty threat. The world had seen what could happen when a prophet in the order of Elisha or Elijah made up their mind. Jonah was trained by the prophetic oracles "gold medallists" of his day. God was not about to let this itinerant scholar of a man sit on some proverbial back side of the desert while the world went to hell in a hand basket. God did not believe in wasting lives.

My Sinister Night of the Soul

By the time Rick and I had shared the 'news' about by my precarious health condition and prayed together as a family, we needed to send the younger children to bed. Everyone was pretty exhausted and tomorrow was a school day. The house grew quiet but as the evening wore on, the peace I had known earlier began to evaporate like the morning mist. The walls seemed to be closing in. An intense battle was beginning to rage in my soul.

In the blackness of the night, my mind felt torment and the abandonment that I had known as a child. "The terrors of death' that David talked about in Psalms, seemed to wrap their icy clutches around my soul. I had never experience this depth of fear before or perhaps since, as I did that night. While the family seemed to sleep peacefully, I tossed and turned relentlessly. What was happening to me?

My whole body seemed to be crawling with agitation. Was it with the sickness or something else more sinister? Suddenly, I began to shake uncontrollably all over. Sleep fled. I arose and went into the menacing darkness of the living room. Again and again this heinous evil seemed to penetrate to the depths of my soul. I felt as if death's grim reaper himself was visiting me. A chilling voice seemed to whisper,

"Where is your God now that you are in our clutches?"

All I could do was to lay prostrate on the carpet in the family room and weep. Why had God forsaken me? What had I done to deserve this? I was not a wicked person. I worked hard to be a good mother and wife. I screamed out to God as questions and thoughts flooded my mind. "Why have you abandoned me? What have I ever done to deserve this?

Help me, Oh my God. Do not leave me alone, now. Do not let me die!"

I buried my face in the carpet and sobbed harder than I had ever in my life. I am sure that I am not the only person that has ever felt abandoned by God. Sometime it seems that even though you do everything right it still turns out wrong. Do you have the resources in your spiritual inventory to prepare when the bottom falls out of your life? As I lay prostrate on my family room carpet, a name came into my mind, 'Darlene.'

It was the name of my sister. I rose to call Darlene on the telephone. I awakened her but she was more than willing to talk even though it was very late. She had been informed of my circumstances by our older sister Leilani. She and I conversed for a long time. Then she began to pray. Oh, what blessed comfort she was on that sinister night when the enemy plagued my tormented soul.

Soon we both became still and quiet as a tangible peace began to invade our space. We felt surrounded, as though invisible guardian angels were trying to make their presence known. The electrifying atmosphere filled our beings and became more prevalent than that sinister oppressive feeling. The demons of doubt, disbelief and fear had been driven off and replaced by hope, faith and love rang. Darlene spoke these words,

"Eileen, I don't understand it but again and again I hear in my spirit. God keeps saying, "All is well, all is well…all is well…!"

My Spiritual Deliver had come. We knew were not alone. We had experienced God's angelic visitors who lifted us out of desperate and a miry dungeon of circumstances. Although I knew the journey would be long, we also knew we would prevail. A sense of peace and love as I had never known enveloped us that evening and left us wanting to learn more.

Keith Holliday has an album that captures this type of encounter with God in a series of worship songs he has simply called, "Face to Face." The album is named for experience that Moses had when he spoke face to face with God in Exodus 33:11 and the glory of God enveloped him. So this was what the Glory of God felt like! Awesome!

Weeks earlier I had attended a service at Carpenter's Home Church in Lakeland, Florida. After hanging up the phone with my sister, I played a tape from the service. It was the only album that I had ever purchased that so captured the presence and glory of God. Since then I have found others.

The music filled the night air as I continued to lie on the carpet. Then, a man with a strange South African accent read scriptures that flooded my barren aching soul and gave me hope. The words seemed to come straight from the throne room of God.

> *There was a thirsty woman who was reaching for the well. Then she met the Master. Her joy no tongue can tell. He told her of the water that she could drink and then, because of its great power, she would never thirst again. Come to the water. There is a vast supply.*

John 4:7-26

Whenever I played the song about the woman and worshiped God, I would experience God's Spirit and wonderful heavenly peace. To my amazement it didn't matter what the place was either, as soon as that music went on, it would flood whatever room I was in. It was like lighting heavenly incense that ushered in the glory of God. The aromatic presence of God would permeate every nook and crevice of the room along with my heart and soul. Repeatedly, I put on the tape on and worshipped, so His presence would come.

The realm of the Spirit is truly beyond the human mind's ability to understand or even fully express. But it is real. I experienced it and so can you! God is no respecter of persons. What He allowed me to experience anyone can experience.

Each individual is so special. I have four children, each unique and as a parent I treasure my relationship with them. It is so important to know each child, one on one or in a face to face encounter. They may share the same genes and have family similarities but they are very different. Would God, the true Divine Parent, create anything less?

Like a Kentucky bloodhound on the scent of a wild fox, I would not be denied. I wanted God to show me as much as I could understand. I was in for the learning experience of a lifetime. As an individual begins to worship and focus on God, the very Presence of God will permeate every part of your being until it drives off every devil of fear and dispels every shadow of doubt. The wonderful presence of God Himself will linger on and on, like the essence and aroma of some wonderful perfume. It will fill and spread throughout the room until all that remains is the fragrance of Him. It is the most wonderful thing a person can experience. To me it is amazing that God desires to have this kind of relationship with His creation, everyday, ordinary people like you and me and yet I am so grateful. Having this type intense encounter with God is the only thing that can get you through something as difficult as what I experienced.

In the weeks to come, I would come to know and understand what the spiritual significance of water from the well. I could well relate to the desperate woman's condition, from the scriptures in John's gospel. I understood the weariness of the woman because I was in the same predicament. The story was speaking about a woman from the Bible who had a spiritual encounter at a drinking well with the Master, Jesus Christ and because of His heavenly words of revelation, her barren soul became peaceful.

The Christian music was from the Lakeland church service and belonged to a preacher named Dr. Rodney Howard-Browne. In the months and years to come whenever the pain of treatment was too great, the circumstances seemed insurmountable or the trial overwhelming, I would simply play the tape and my spirit would be buoyed up with faith, peace and joy. I clutched the tape and held it during surgery, even though technically I was not supposed to carry anything. That tape accompanied me to all procedures and with it I experienced and connected to a realm of heaven that I didn't know existed.

So this was what the term meant by living water that the song had sung about. The water was an expression or code word that represented a person's spirit. As the music played and the person's spirit worshipped God, it was as if your soul had access to a river that supplied the deepest and purest water. This heavenly hose would hook up to the endless ocean of supply from God. Who willingly will empty Himself into your waiting vessel. No longer fearful, barren or dry but one's spiritual thirst can be filled, quenched and satisfied.

I imagined myself drifting down a stream that carried me into this mighty river of God's presence and love. Whenever I needed it there it was. No matter how challenging the trial this love carried and flooded my spirit, removing every fear by overflowing me with the tangible presence of God's love. All I had to do was simply close my eyes pray and begin to worship God. Then God would strengthen me with enough peace and joy to overshadow any difficulty. The presence and peace of God became more real than the reality of this world.

Although the next two weeks were somewhat of a blur, there were certain things that I can never forget. God has given the human mind an amazing ability to blocking out unpleasant things as a survival mechanism. I am thankful that much of the suffering, discomfort and pain was not remembered so that I am not continually tormented by my experiences of the past and yet certain scenes are indelibly seared into my consciousness.

Elie Wiesel, in his 1986 Nobel Prize winning book called *Night* recounts his horrific experiences as a young boy in the infamous concentration camp called Auschwitz. He said the following, "Never, never shall I forget these things even if I am condemned to live as long as God Himself. Never !"

Although I could never consider my experiences on a par with Mr. Weisel, I can certainly relate to the part about never forgetting certain things. After receiving the "news" of my precarious health condition, my husband dutifully checked me into the hospital at five a.m. the following day. What followed was not exactly what I would call a fun filled day. Each procedure was followed by a test that seemed worse than the prior one. Moreover, there was such a contrast between the staff and me. While they remained calm, cool and sometimes indifferent, I was intimidated by unfamiliar surroundings, frightened by painful procedures and nervously overwhelmed by the weighty decisions that I had to make in a split second that involved my future.

Sometimes I was not completely sure of the consequences of choices that I had to make at what seemed like the drop of the hat. How would all of this ultimately affect not only me but also my family? I teetered the gamut of emotions from being hot-tempered, to anxious, for the most part emotionally distraught, "Was the cure worse than the disease?" I wondered.

The first major procedure was done by Dr. Xavier Cannella, a well-respected vascular surgeon also a close friend of Dr. Jim Etheridge. This involved inserting a plastic tube into my throat, so that dialysis could be performed. I was fortunate to have, in my opinion, not only one of the most qualified doctors in his field, but a wonderful and caring physician. What a blessing to begin with someone of his caliber and expertise.

After asking me if I understood what was about to be done to me I caustically replied, "You're about to slice my throat."

He raised his eyebrows but smiled and nodded in agreement and waited for me to explain to him the rest of the scenario that was about to transpire. That was not precisely what was done but in my eyes that was about the gist of it. A small opening was cut into my neck to reach the large vein located there. Carefully, Dr. Cannella pushed long plastic tubes into the arteries that traveled toward the heart. Two tubes were needed to both remove and return the blood simultaneously to my body. Two tubes were necessary because one tube had to move the blood up the neck to the dialysis machine to be cleaned while the other tube was needed to return the cleansed blood to my body. This process would continue for about three hours until all my blood was finally clean. Everyone seemed so pleased with the preparatory surgeries thus far. That is everyone but me! To me it all sounded *gross*!

As soon as these tubes were positioned in my neck Dr. Cannella efficiently sowed them permanently in place by a couple of small, neat stitches.

"Permanently, why permanently, who is going to take these out?" I thought to myself!"

Everything was happening so fast there was no opportunity to ask more questions. Oh, how those little stitches pulled and interfered with even the tiniest movement that I made whether it was eating drinking or even resting. Furthermore, the pain and discomfort of having this type of foreign thing in the throat area was incredible.

No one appeared concerned with my vanity as I thought, "How many marks or scars will this leave?"

Now, I almost blush when I think of how foolish I was. How many sick people do you know who are overly concerned about how they look? Before everything was over, I too became less vain than when I began my ordeal. At this point, no comfortable position existed for me to get into. Would I ever be able to find one in the near or distant future? Uncomfortable as this was, nothing could be compared with what lay ahead. Keep in mind that everything was leading *up* to me to receiving that dreaded dialysis treatment, still to come. The staff continuously reminded me that if I refused treatments although painful, nothing could be compared to the horrible consequences that would follow.

When I have the opportunity I sure would like to speak to that *certain committee* that decides to tell the patient the most gruesome details regarding of all that could possibly go wrong with the procedure to the already fearful and confused patient. When I find this group, I would like to ask them why they feel it necessary to torment the already terrified patient. Are they hoping that the information will frighten and intimidate us into succumbing to any and all treatments the staff may suggest? When I find this *certain committee* I would like to give them a piece of my mind. Would it be possible for them to be more humane and create a scenario where detailed information is given in a gentler and caring environment or would that would be too much to ask?

Again, I thought to myself as I looked defiantly at the next nurse but naturally did not say a word, "At least put a more positive spin on the treatments. Lastly give me some hope and faith rather than fear and despair."

Now I realize that perhaps this was done because many of the patients will never recover from what I was about to endure. When the blood can no longer remove waste and fluid, it must be purified artificially to remove poison or it will turn uremic. Further, if the water is not removed from the body, excess water will fill the lungs causing the patient to suffocate and die. I thought on these things during the wee hours of the morning.

Finally

After endless tests and an exhausting morning, I was finally wheeled back to an empty hospital room to await my next ordeal. My only solace was that I was not alone. I put on my tape, remembering that God was with me. What do people do without the comfort of the precious Holy Spirit? To have the wonderful blanket of God's ever present love and peace flood your being and the wonderful Divine assurance that says you are going to make it! A scripture popped into my mind. Another way that God encouraged me was to bring just the right scripture into mind when I needed it most. "For the Lord is good and His mercy does endure for all times." From the hospital bed, I reflected on those timeless words as I looked around the antiseptic hospital room and thought.

Less than twenty-four hours have passed and yet I felt as though I had lived a lifetime since Dr. Alveranga's phone call. My whole life had changed. Would my life ever be normal again?

Chapter Review

1. **Name the enemy of your soul and name the deliverer of your soul.**

    _____

    _____

    _____

Chapter 5

Steering Into the Storm

∘ ∘

Then they called on the Lord and said, "We earnestly pray,
O Lord, do not let us perish on account of this man's life and
do not put (his) innocent blood on us; for Thou, O Lord,
hast done as Thou pleased." So they picked up Jonah, threw
him into the sea, and the sea stopped its raging.

Jonah 1: 14 & 15

A Little Help from My Friends

"Cast me in the sea," Jonah insisted. The sailor's wrung their hands terrified
not knowing what to do but in the end capitulated. They had no choice.
Angry waves crashed over the deck driving the small merchant craft perilously
onward and threatening to rapidly send the crew to a watery grave. Upon
Jonah's insistence they finally hurled him into the depths of the squalling
stormy ocean...and into his destiny.

Instantly, the tempestuous seas stopped rolling and quieted down like a
pacified and contented sleeping baby. It was as though there had never been
a problem. The ocean became as calm as glass.

From time to time, everyone needs a little help from their friends. Jonah
was no exception. But was this the help he needed? One wonders whether this
was a hand up or a step down. The laurel wreath of victory is placed firmly
on the head of the conquering general when in reality it should be placed
at the feet of the faithful army that faithfully secures the victory. I was no
exception. I had many faithful friends, among them Beth James and Audra
Bulin. Early on they gave me tapes by a man named Doug Jones. He was
one of the main instructors at RHEMA Bible Training Center in Oklahoma.

They were simply called "What You Must Understand." I played them until they stretched. But by the time they were worn out, some things were firmly established within my mind and heart.

One such truth was that God wanted me well and healed. First I had to be convinced that God wanted me well; much later, I would have to think about *how to* reach this goal. But for now it was an important start. Earlier and for many weeks, I had been asking God why. Why had He permitted this thing to happen to me? God could not be the author of evil since he was God. Why didn't He prevent this? No answer came.

The realization began to dawn on me that this line of questioning was getting me nowhere. In one sense, asking God why was like those foolish sailors on Jonah's craft who toiled and struggled unsuccessfully to try and row backwards toward the shore. The raging storm persisted. Finally, the terrified the sailors asked Jonah what must be done next to appease his angry God? Although trite and obvious for the reader, that question literary took weeks of listening to Doug Jones before I too was able to wade through to ask the next question. When I did, confusion seemed to cease and the next set of instructions came plainly, "Move forward!"

In a sense Beth and Audra were like those sailors who were used by God to thrust Jonah into the sea. A difficult part of the journey was to relinquish oneself to the storm. An interesting thing happened as a result, although everything appeared out of my control, it soon became apparent that I was firmly and uniquely positioned in God's hands and He *was* in control.

If you are toiling and going nowhere, perhaps it is time to stop looking back towards shore and face the open sea. Stop denying that this is happening. Truly my first step of faith was acceptance! There was a raging storm and I was in the middle of it. And if something was not done immediately then this vessel that I was in, would end up at the bottom of the ocean floor.

When the crew of any vessel senses that a storm is imminent, they must either cast off the rope that attaches them to the pier or cling to the shoreline and risk crashing the vessel onto the rocks. Moving into the open sea is usually a safer option.

Before throwing him overboard, a weary Jonah stood up straight and smoothed down his camel haired cloak with attached leather girdle. Leaning upon his crooked old staff, slowly and carefully he began to spin his tale. Motioning them over with his hands, the sailors moved closer. Meanwhile, in the background the wind and storm howled on. His crackled voice began with an eccentric prophet named Elijah.

A certain king Ahad had a steward named Obadiah. Obadiah hid and fed prophets in a cave while the king's wicked wife Queen Jezebel threatened to destroy all of God's servants. This Phoenician Queen was as bad as the

Disney character called *Cruela Devil*!   This story can be found in I Kings 21:1-23. Israel's King Ahab lusted after a particular vineyard on the side of a hill in Jezreel located not too far from his palace. Because the land was his inheritance, it was against the law for Naboth to sell the land to Naboth.

When a depressed Ahab whined to his wicked wife Jezebel, she decided to hatch an evil plan. She wrote letters to the local officials accusing innocent Naboth of blaspheming God. The punishment under Jewish law was stoning for Naboth and his family. This cruel act along with so many others marked the couple's undoing. As judgment for this treachery God gave the prophet Elijah a prophecy for the couple. Elijah never saw this come to pass but it was finally realized under the prophetic ministry of the next prophet Elisha.

> *The dogs shall eat Jezebel in the district of Jezreel.*

> I Kings 21:23

When God had seen enough from Ahab's evil house, He told the prophet Elisha to select a new King of Israel. Military captain Jehu eliminated the evil queen Jezebel by riding in a chariot to Jezebel's tower.

> *And he (Jehu) said, "Throw her (Jezebel) down," so they threw*
> *her down, and some of her blood was sprinkled on the wall and*
> *on the horses, and he trampled her under foot. And they went*
> *to bury her, and they found no more of her than the skull and*
> *the feet and the palms of her hands.*

> II Kings 9:33

Thus Jezebel died according to the original prophecy given by Elijah. Revenge upon wicked Queen Jezebel was complete. Crime did not pay. The sailors listening to Jonah's tale were probably wide eyed as they decided. "Never has there been a God like the God Jonah serves." Imagine the look on the sailors face. How horrible to be eaten by dogs or worse. All of this must have terrified the sailors as they noticed the massive waves rolling over the bow of their ship. Jonah's God was not to be trifled with.

By this time probably someone had gotten the old man a rough wooden crate to rest upon. Maybe another sailor filled a chalice of red wine from the captain's choice supply. If they were going down, these superstitious sailors would at least have a heavenly advocate to fight for them. More sailors continued to leave their posts in shifts so they could listen.

No longer was there disgust and scorn for the old prophet. As the saying goes, calamity makes for strange bed fellows. When the vessel careened sideways, the men and the captain rushed forward to keep the old man from losing his balance and placed a dry canvas across his shoulders to keep him dry. All during the night, sailors traded shifts for a turn at listening while other mariners toiled in the storm trying to get the vessel to stabilize, so they could hear the rest of the story.

No one could tell when it happened but somehow the atmosphere on the ship began to change. For one brief moment, during the blackness of the night a holy hush descended with an electrified Holy presence as Jonah communicated to the sailors about the Holy of Holies in the temple of Solomon. Faith replaced fear, hope had replaced desperation and love displaced distrust and prejudice. Peace and silence reigned. The toughest men had moist eyes and humbled countenances. Former rough and cursing sailors traded a turn at listening to Jonah while an eerie moonless night watch gave way to the dawn of another stormy day.

The rebel Jonah was no more. Pastor Jonah had returned to shepherd a poor and lost humanity replete with pierced ears, scarred faces and tattooed bodies. This strange flock with brightened countenances now reflected the Father's love. Although it didn't seem to fit with Jonah's theology, he saw they too were children of God. Grace has abounded to the very least of these. For a moment everyone had forgotten where they were and how terrifying the storm at sea was. Where God's presence abides there is grace no matter how difficult the circumstances and estranged the group.

Old Jonah had many more wonderful tales for the sailors. We can't be sure of how many Bible stories Jonah told to the men on that fateful voyage but we know it was enough to convince them that his God was the one true God. We can imagine that Jonah looked into the velvety black eyes of a curly haired youth with ebony hair and continued his teaching from II Kings 2:11-15.

Finally, at the end of his life, as if a life time of miracles wasn't enough, Elijah was taken by whirlwind up to heaven in a fiery chariot. This was God's way of giving Elijah a stamp of approval for a difficult job well done. Elisha, prophetic understudy of Elijah, stood by watching. Elisha was trained for his job by serving Elijah. According to the Bible, he rent (rips) his (secular) clothes in twain (two) and immediately took up the mantle (prophetic clothing and calling) of Elijah, his former boss, teacher and mentor. Upon returning home, Elisha needed to cross the Jordan River, he struck the river with his new mantle and split the river in two as his predecessor Moses had done. No less than fifty servants witnessed the scene of splitting the Jordan River in two and you can be sure that it made a favorable impression. It was abundantly clear to all those watching, that the mandate and authority of prophet, now fell to Elisha.

Elisha, son of Shaphat is here, who use to pour water on the hands of Elijah.

II Kings 3:11.

Now a certain Shunamite woman had given a room and meal to Elisha and his servant as they passed though the town. When the prophet asked how he could repay the woman for her kindness she declined, saying that she was well taken care of by her elderly husband. Gahazi, the servant who traveled with Elisha noted that she had no child. He told Elisha that when her husband died, she would be left alone with none to provide for her. So Elisha gave her a prophecy saying that she would have a child the following year. The child came just as Elisha had promised. Years later, the boy fell ill and died. The grief stricken mother saddled a donkey and took the dead child back to the prophet. The prophet stretched himself over the lad, breathed into him and raised the boy from the dead. II Kings 4:8-37. These 'prophets of old, men of renown,' as the Bible called them, did not have superstar status. They worked side by side, mentoring their younger prophets and when miracles occurred, their numbers swelled. Many a young man wanted to gain this type of notoriety. With all of these new students, dormitories had to be constructed. One day, one of the rookie prophets lost his borrowed ax in the river. Elisha recovered the ax by having it float to the top.

> *Now the sons of the prophets said to Elisha, "Behold now, the place before you where we are living is too limited for us." "Please, let us go to the Jordan, and each of us take from there a beam, and let us make a place there for ourselves where we may live." So he said, "Go." So he went with them; and when they came to the Jordan, they cut down trees. But as one was felling a beam, the axe head fell into the water; and he cried out and said, "Alas, my master! For it was borrowed." Then the man of God said, "Where did it fall?" And when he showed him the place, he cut off a stick, and threw it in there, and made the iron float.*

II Kings 6:1-6

Imagine an impressionable Jonah, growing up, hearing and witnessing these miraculous acts and then receiving his ministry charge, 'to go and do likewise'? Would a young Jonah, have closed his door and practiced the 'water splitting' feat with the bedding from his dormitory room? When he did he found out that miracles may look easier than they sounded! For God getting and training good help, was as difficult then as it is today. Judgment also was an integral part of the prophet's world. An example of this was Gahazi servant of the prophet Elisha.

> *Now the king (Ben-hadad king of Syria) was talking with Gehazi, the servant of the man of God, saying, "Please relate to me all the great things that Elisha has done."*

II Kings 8:4

Being a servant then as it is today meant that you were mentored or next in line for the job of prophet, but only if you passed all the tests. Gehazi, servant to Elisha was rendered with a horrible judgment of leprosy by his master Elisha because he lied and was greedy. Many questions came to my mind as I thought about Gehazi. Could he have been a past friend, colleague or even a roommate of Jonah? More importantly, when Gehazi blew it, was Jonah next in line for the vacated position? And when had God spoken to him about the Ninevites? Did Jonah tell his fellow prophets or did he just keep it to himself and flee?

After telling all those Jonah's wrinkled hands stroke his long, white beard. Sitting upon the old wooden bench he rested an affectionate and weary arm on a young lad with black velvet eyes and curly hair. The young man looked back into those grandfatherly brown twinkling eyes and asked.

"Sir, will we all die now? We are not afraid, if we can go to your God in heaven. We believe that He is the true God of the heavens." A salty tear must have splashed down the face of the worn out prophet as he told them the final message of how the word of the Lord came to him about the Ninevites and how he disobeyed and ended up in the storm.

"All of this trouble is because of me," Jonah explained. With a wrinkled brow, he looked into their faces and resolutely decided to save these poor wretched lost lambs, who now only want desperately to please this old man and the God he served.

"There is no God like the God of Jonah. He is terrible and awesome and worthy to be feared and revered," the crew decided.

One by one they decided they would make vows to the God of Jonah so they came up to him, no longer hostile and without a word begin to lay certain things at the old man's feet. First the brawny rough faced Phoenician put down a beautiful ornately decorated vase with birds and flowers. Next the swarthy and brawny Egyptian removed his golden earrings and bracelet. A fierce Assyrian laid down an alabaster jar with precious myrrh. Even the captain has removed an amethyst ring. Last of all the boy with velvet black eyes disappeared and returned with a breastplate of pure gold. Loot fit for the great God that Jonah served. Laying the treasures at his feet, Jonah decides on a plan to save them.

"After all they have done no wrong. It is my fault that they are in all of this mess." He decided. A lone tear glistens down the cheek of the old man. "Without the shedding of blood there is no remission for sin," his priestly conscience reminds him.

Now as never before he has seen that the compassion of his God also rested on more than just Hebrew lambs. He knew what he must do to save the life of the very precious crew but would his courage fail him as it had before?

Dynamic Duo: Ken and Barbie

Through my endless night of the soul, I had learned an important lesson. God had not abandoned me. I knew that no matter how difficult the trial He would remain and be there if I searched for Him with my whole heart, all of my strength and mind.

Clinging to the words *"all is well,"* from my sister Darlene and surrounded by the music that had taken me through the night, the love and peace of God returned. The music comforted my soul and kept peace in my mind. Yes, pain and fear would try and regain a foothold but then I recalled the words to the song "Her joy no words can ever tell" and let them play in my mind so the peace returned. To this day I can recite and hum all the music with a little prompting. It was my security blanket through Hell like the favorite worn Teddy bear of a child.

It was after lunchtime and I hadn't had a bite to eat since the day before. Maybe it was endless tests and procedures or perhaps it was the anxiety. The nurse brought in some unknown pills for me to take. Mechanically I swallowed. Quickly her footsteps disappeared down the hall corridor. The nasty medicines on an empty stomach made my stomach queasy. I ended up throwing up everything all over myself.

With tubes in my neck and the soreness of the surgery fresh from the morning, I laboriously climbed out of bed. Stitches tore at my neck as I tried to clean myself up in the bathroom and prepare for whatever the next ordeal was.

With the unknown dialysis treatment looming ahead of me, there wasn't a moment to lose. I was told it could last anywhere from three to four hours. While emotionally bracing myself for the next ordeal, I cleaned up so I wouldn't be smelly and wet. Stiffly and carefully, with tubes and stitches still in my neck, I managed to carefully put one arm in the hospital gown and then the other. I was trying hard not to disturb any of the attached apparatus so it wouldn't pull or hurt too bad.

"Better to do things myself," I thought, "if I asked assistance, who knows how long I will have to wait." Looking back now I know that I was still clinging to what little pride and dignity I had left.

Meanwhile, outside the bathroom door I heard a voice barking orders at me.

The orderly hollered, "Look, if you don't get out here right this minute I'm going to write down that you are refusing treatment."

"I'll try to get out as soon as I can." I weakly answered from the bathroom. Apparently I was too slow. By the time I was out of the bathroom she was gone. I finished cleaning up…carefully. The next thing I knew, a nurse came marching into the room with the attendant and a piece of paper to sign. I climbed back into bed while the nurse demanded with arms folded. "Are you refusing treatment?" You know what will happen to you if you choose this course of action?" If so, you need to sign this.

"There's been some sort of misunderstanding. All I wanted to do was to clean myself up from my accident before treatment." I explained.

With this confusion cleared up, a new order went out. One phone call later a different orderly was wheeling me down another endless hospital corridor to the dialysis treatment room. I was about to find out what this next dreaded treatment entailed.

A quiet darkness descended on us as we entered a room off the hospital corridor that read *Dialysis*. My throat felt dry and tight. I tried to rally my strength with a weak smile. Secretly, I was terrified. I clutched my hidden tape player in the folds from the hospital gown and blanket and prayed.

"Are you Eileen Austin," the technician queried?

"Yes." Regretfully I acknowledged her as my eyes slowly adjusted to the darkness. There were more human forms than I had originally noticed.

"Why was everything so dark, and not bright as the other treatment rooms?" I thought. More technicians and nurses attended other patients. These patients were attached to the machines by thin crimson lines. The lines then descended from their arms to two wheels that seemed to rotate on the face of huge machines. Around and around the wheels went. Stiff white sheets held patients resting motionless upon bed after bed in neat rows.

A horrible thought crept into mind as I wondered if they were still alive.

Slowly the wheels carried the same crimson lines from the front to a small crimson pump on the side of the machine. These crimson pumps would empty and fill, empty and fill all the while pulsating with a systematic rhythm like that of a human heart. Later, I found out that the crimson lines were really clear and that it was *red* blood coursing through the lines. I was also accurate about the pulsating blood.

It was the beat of the human heart because the blood also carried the pulse from the heart. As the blood pulsated again and again a scripture from Leviticus 17:11 came to mind. The life is in the blood. The life is in the blood. What life you may ask? According to the Word of God... all life!

The actual treatment room held about eight beds. The nurse who I will call Barbie later explained that it was kept dark because many of the patients like to sleep during treatment.

Sleep? I thought. "Were they kidding? How could anyone sleep while they were being dialyzed? I soon would learn why the patients slept. When you thought about it, it was really made a lot of sense. As the life blood of the individual was literally and slowly emptied out and returned it would only stand to reason that the exchange would tire the body out. Sleeping truly was the best way to handle the ordeal. In a few treatments I too would learn to be more relaxed and even casual about the whole thing. At this moment, however, I couldn't imagine being that relaxed about anything.

My mind reasoned, "Surely, this is just temporary and I am dreaming. Soon, I will wake up and all of this bad nightmare will be over."

But it wasn't and I was there to stay. Looking around I noticed the walls were lined with various apparatus like oxygen tanks and other things that I couldn't identify. I wondered are these life supports necessary? I would soon find out that one can never be too casual or comfortable with dialysis because even the slightest human or machine can mess up and cause great chaos with the life of a patient. Before my two very long years of dialysis treatment was over I would get many opportunities to see how precarious life can be for the dialysis patient.

My turn came next. Bidding goodbye to the transport person, a male and female nurse approached me to prepare me for dialysis. After the previous experience in the hospital room I wasn't sure what to expect. But these two nurses turned out to be extremely kind, patient and qualified. First they prepared the machine and hooked up the new plastic lines and pump which was actually the artificial kidney. Next everything was checked to make sure I was ready to do my run as they call dialysis.

Barbie made sure my bed was sufficiently propped up so that I could watch everything. And watch I did, like a hawk! Not that I could be helpful in any way. Next, they cleaned the graft or access in my neck as it was called meticulously and super sanitized so no germs could enter. Then my graft was hooked up to the plastic lines and I was off and running so to speak.

So this is the fearsome dialysis? No big deal. But I would change my opinion of all of this later sooner rather than later.

Just What Are My Options

Just as I was beginning to relax, a nervous and irritated doctor appeared out of nowhere, insisting that I sign the consent paper so that the staff could begin processing paper work for a transplant. As he continued to stick the paper in front of me, urging me to sign it, I firmly resisted. He was not happy with me when I asked him to come back when I was off dialysis and in a better position to talk,

"Just what are my options, doc?"

He said, "Are you kidding? You have no options! You have had kidney failure."

I was never given another opportunity to respond. Clearly he was agitated. He just spun around and marched out of the room leaving as quickly as he entered.

The noise of his heels grew softer as he disappeared and headed down the corridor leaving me alone with my thoughts. Maybe to him there weren't any options for this stubborn woman but I still needed time to discuss things with my husband, family and pray. Mostly pray, that was the principle thing that I needed to do. Maybe to him, I had no options but in my mind I was about to embark on a great adventure with God to find out exactly what my options were. When he stormed out, secretly I was glad. They didn't know who they were dealing with and they weren't going to push me around.

On further reflection, and though I hate to admit it, this doctor was correct and trying to spare me of great difficulty in the days that lay ahead. He understood what I did not, that there are numerous health difficulties, torment and suffering that accompany the normal dialysis patient. However, if the individual is not psychologically ready to go the next step than they are not in a receptive frame of mind. Many healthy dialysis patients never opt to have a transplant because of the risks involved. For a long time after that doctor left I was upset at his callous bedside manner. He didn't respect me enough to sit down and explain certain things to me. How could he be so insensitive? Later I would meet this doctor under different circumstances and found him to be one of the most loving, wonderful and caring doctors you could ever meet. It never occurred to me that they too could be stressed in having to care for patients like myself.

My first dialysis treatment had finally come to an end. My male nurse, Ken, and I chatted easily. He reminded me of a great big teddy bear. This middle age, ex-army medic explained to me precisely what the dialysis machines and treatment were all about. This would not be the first time that I was blessed and saved by a person who had been given their experience in the military. I have found him and the other former medics to be some one of the most caring individuals that worked on me. Is it because their training is under intense condition normally? At the time, I really wasn't that interested in the whole process but at least my mind was off the procedure and he took the time to connect with me.

Although the idea of them taking out my blood was repulsive I still listened. After all I was a captive audience and attached to the machine. It wasn't as though I could get up and leave now could I? He explained that when kidneys are no longer capable of filtering and cleaning blood, they need the assistance of an artificial kidney. This artificial kidney was a tube that held hundreds of tiny fibers that filtered and cleaned my blood. Filters hooked up to the machine would also be hooked to the access lines surgically sewn into my neck. Later on, when I was able to go home, I jokingly said to my daughter that she had a mother that had to be plugged in every other day.

While one line took out the blood out, the artificial kidney filtered and removed impurities from my blood. The other line carried the cleaned blood back into my body. The entire process occurred slowly and under extreme precision and caution, lest in an unsanitary circumstance create danger to the patient. If extreme caution not taken, a slight infection could occur damaging the heart or worse possibly killing the patient.

During the next two years, and after many treatments, I experienced the best and worst case scenario. Taking blood from a human body is a tricky and dangerous procedure with possibly a thousand things going wrong. Because of the difficulty and expense of this procedure, in some countries like England where the medicine is socialized, they do not even bother to treat patients older than fifty. My treatment had gone well because Ken and Barbie (as I nicknamed my two wonderful nurses) were caring and skilled at what they did. When it was finally over, I was extremely relieved and hungry! I wanted to hug them and cry all at the same time. The competence of this exceptional dynamic duo marked my first time on dialysis and for that I would always be grateful. Night came and this time, two companions of pain and anxiety tried to bed down with me again.

Chapter Review

1. **What was one of the stories that the prophet Jonah told to the sailors?**

   _____

   _____

   _____

2. **How did the sailors respond to the stories that Jonah told about God?**

    _____

    _____

    _____

Chapter 6

Living Sacrifice

○ ○

So they picked up Jonah and threw him into the sea, and the
sea stopped its raging. Then the men feared the Lord greatly,
and they offered a sacrifice to the Lord and made vows. And
the Lord appointed a great fish to swallow Jonah and Jonah
was in the stomach of the fish three days and three nights.

Jonah 1:15-17

Clueless

It is difficult to imagine that the prophet actually slept peacefully up until
the storm began. Unfortunately, as amazing as this sounds many of us are
more like Jonah than we care to admit. We are clueless to the lost humanity
surrounding us and oblivious to those desperately rowing around us until
God fingers us to start talking like Jonah did. Is that what it takes to take
this life-giving message to a lost and dying world? We have the solution to
peoples' problems but what a chore it is to get us talking!

The blessing is that God loves us enough ***not*** to let our vessels to go down
until we have an opportunity to redeem ourselves. Perhaps this is why we
experience such trials on earth. Maybe they are not just to make life difficult,
but are to get us to do the things that we ought to have done in the first place.

The crew rowed Jonah around and around in circles, while the vessel
tossed and turned. Finally he was thrown overboard, but that was not the
end to his desperate trials but merely the beginning. God had gotten Jonah's
attention but now He had to instill a proper fear and respect to insure that
Jonah followed through, step by step.

How many of us are this stubborn, that it takes a shipwreck to finally get us going in the right direction. As the saying goes talk is cheap while actions speak louder than words. Anyone can promise anything under the duress of the moment but when the pressure is off is the person willing to be obedient or does God have to allow another series of difficult circumstance on order to follow through and get the job done? The spirit is willing on Sunday but the flesh is oh so weak on Monday.

It is not enough to be willing to die, sometimes *that* is the easy way out. God wants us to be living sacrifices. Unfortunately, for many of us that means more character adjustments in the crucible of difficult circumstances. We all have more than a little bit of stubborn in our backbone.

Just when our worst fears are realized and we are about to justifiably ready to condemn Jonah, he does something amazing. He has this startling epiphany and attempts to correct his deplorable attitude. He acknowledged responsibility for the storm to the crew, explaining that all this trouble had come upon them because of *him*. Our reluctant prophet communicates God's mission to the mariners. Had love and compassion finally found Jonah? We will never know but he does appear to have more than a passing concern of safety for his "new friends."

> *"For I know that on account of me this great storm has come upon you."*

> Jonah 1:12

After taking responsibility for the catastrophe, the prophet had done a one hundred and eighty degree turn. He had finally seen the light and we, the reading audience breathe a sigh of relief. This is much more comfortable to live with. Imagine if preachers and Christians took responsibility for their actions.

When the Christians take their place in society everyone benefits. But often instead of being salt and light, Christians appear to blunder more than sinners, acting more like drunken sailors on a furlough on some distant shore. The trickledown effect of these thoughtless actions adversely impacts others. Some Christians even have the nerve to play the blame game. With their #1 song being "the devil made me do it …the devil made me do it."

When Jonah connected with the rough sailors, he began to care about what happened to them more than in saving his own neck. Self less instead of selfish, Jonah redeemed himself and became a hero. What caused such a dramatic turn of events? Had his guilty conscience finally gotten to him? It must have. At least enough to have the sailors 'heave him ho.'

In the twinkling of the eye, the sailors hurled him into the raging sea. But our hero had been so naughty up to this point that we hardly even notice this act of nobility and courage. In all my years of church attending and hearing various sermons about Jonah, never was his sacrifice or the men throwing him overboard, the focus of a story. Saving the life of the crew is almost a footnote. But what a footnote! When was the last time you were willing to own up to your mistakes in such a magnanimous fashion? Still more amazing is the crew. They scriptures state that they were reluctant to throw him overboard?

Could they really be interested in the fate of one old man or were they too just being selfish and concerned about further wrath from the powerful Deity that Jonah served? Had he convinced them that his God was the true God and that he indeed was Jehovah's prophet? Apparently, he had, because formerly we read in

Jonah 1:5 "every man prayed to his god." In other words they sacrificed to no one particular god but by **Jonah 1:16** it states, **"The men feared God greatly and offered a sacrifice in addition to vows."** What had transpired between verse 5 and verse 16? Simply put, **revelation that only fiery preaching can bring!**

Imagine the sailors praying to Jonah's God for mercy! Even though Jonah's message was brief, God had used the simplicity of preaching to precipitate a radical change in these men. They saw their spiritual blindness and moved from darkness to light. May I suggest that when Christians finally come into their own, and act right, they become salt and others around them are blessed, impacted and radically changed.

Economics has given us a timeless principle. When something is purchased, a price has been paid. A cost was involved. Who would pay the sacrifice if not Jonah? In the same way, who will pay if not the Christian? What one gives up or pays for future generations is called investment (plus interest); by the same token, what one takes from the future at the expense of the present is called debt. Each person makes the decision whether to consume or invest in the present.

Why did Jonah have to sacrifice himself in such a final way? As a prophet Jonah had a basic understanding about God's nature and what remedy was required for balance to be restored.

What Jonah Understood

Then the Lord passed by in front of him (Moses) and proclaimed, "The Lord, the Lord God, compassionate and gracious, slow to anger, and abounding in loving kindness and truth; Who

keeps loving kindness for thousands, who forgives iniquity, transgressions and sin; yet He will by no means leave the guilty unpunished, visiting the iniquity of fathers on the children and on the grandchildren to the third and fourth generations." And Moses made haste to bow low toward the earth and worshiped.

Exodus 34:6-8

There is a wonderful book called *The Land of the Bible* by authors Packer, Tenney and White. Page 114 contains some interesting information on animal sacrifice. It reminds the modern audience that although animal sacrifice in religion appears repulsive to us, in ancient times it was a method of worship. Blood has always been synonymous with life. Later on in this chapter, we will look at the value of and reason for, blood sacrifice. It is common knowledge that human sacrifice was widely practiced by the nations that surrounded the Hebrews.

Since human sacrifice was strictly forbidden by God, an animal was substituted. Perhaps that is one reason that Judaism and ultimately Christianity were eagerly embraced by surrounding nations in the New World. They no longer required the sacrifice of their children or loved ones to appease an angry God for their shortcomings.

The first sacrifice for sin ever offered by God was in the Garden of Eden when Adam and Eve sinned.

And the Lord God made garments of skin for Adam and his wife Eve and clothed them.

Genesis 3: 21

The sons of Adam and Eve continued this family tradition started by God.

Abel brought the firstlings of his flock and of their fat portions but Cain brought an offering of the fruit of the ground. And the Lord had regard for Abel and his offering but for Cain He had no regard.

Genesis 5: 3-5

Jonah understood that as a prophet of the Most High God, sacrifice for man's sin was necessary to avert impending calamities from God. The old covenant consisted of an eye for an eye and a tooth for a tooth. This would all change when Jesus came on the scene in the New Testament but for now, the Old Testament covenant was still in effect.

Some of the animals offered for man's crime were oxen, cattle, goats and birds. The kind of animal offered depended on the severity of the crime. Whatever the animal, it had to be perfect, worthy of sacrifice. We begin to understand the problem that Jonah had when his sin was discovered on the boat. A sacrifice was needed to appease God for the sinful acts of both the crew and especially Jonah but where could this sacrifice be found when the sea was raging? They were desperate. So Jonah got creative.

Jonah was a prophet. Participating in the slaughter of animals was nothing new. Offering up of the sacrifices for the sins of the people was the meat and potatoes so to speak of his job. As the ship tossed and turned, he suddenly had an idea, a solution but would it work? When he told the men what to do, they protested vigorously and objected but finally gave in. There was no other solution in sight and then again what if this would make Jonah's God even angrier.

There was just no getting around the raging sea. In the end they placated the old eccentric prophet and did as he wished. They send him to His God albeit reluctantly! Some commentaries seem to suggest that the crew were only doing this because they feared Jonah's God but I think that there was more to it than that.

What a sight they must have been that fateful day, those rough and ready sailors with moist eyes and strong backs, heaving ho. "And a one and a two and a three" and in Jonah went, down into a black, raging sea. Down, down, down to a watery grave. They lean over the slippery deck of the careening vessel and watch the man disappear. The surface of the water broke and then quickly closed around Jonah. The men wondered what would happen next. Glug, glug, glug, Jonah dropped from their sight like a rock and then something happened just a Jonah had said.

Moments after hurling Jonah in the ocean, a miracle occurs. The waves quieted down and the ocean appeared to be glass again. Could there be any doubt in any of their minds now? God was indeed the true God and Jonah was His servant. Immediately they humbly bowed themselves on the deck of the ship and begged God to show them mercy. According to the scripture they even made good on all their promised vows.

> *Then the men feared the Lord greatly, and they offered a sacrifice to the Lord and made vows.*

Jonah 1:16

For Jonah this selfless act of courage won him a place of honor in the chronicles of super heroes, God's Hall of Fame in Hebrews 12. Although we tend to focus on his disobedience, we must remember that God has always been and will always be loving, merciful, a 'forgive and forget' kind of God. From then on when Jonah is mentioned in scripture, it is with compliments and never in condemnation. How like God that is and *how unlike us!* God even compares Jonah in subsequent parts of the Bible with none other than Jesus Himself. It is our weak human nature from Adam that dwells on the earlier and more disobedient pages of the Book of Jonah.

Let us also remember the entire city repented, including the king. Jonah's message caused the city to be spared even the animals! If this kind of full scale success had been enjoyed by a modern day preacher it certainly would have been covered by the T.B.N. or the Christian news network at the very least.

But He (Jesus) answered and said to them, "An evil and adulterous generation craves for a sign; and no sign shall be given to it but the sign of Jonah the prophet; For just as Jonah was three days and three nights in the belly of the sea monster; so shall the son of Man be three days and three nights in the heart of the earth. The men of Nineveh shall stand up with this generation at the judgment, and shall condemn it because they repented at the preaching of Jonah; and behold something greater than Jonah is here.

Mathew 12: 39-41

And as the crowds were increasing, He began to say, "This generation is a wicked generation; it seeks for a sign and yet no sign shall be given to it but the sign of Jonah. For as Jonah became a sign to the Ninevites, so shall the Son of Man be to this generation. The Queen of the South shall rise up with the men of this generation at the judgment and condemn them, because she came from the ends of the earth to hear the wisdom of Solomon; and behold, something greater than Solomon is here. "The men of Nineveh shall stand up with this generation at the judgment and condemn it, because they repented at the preaching of Jonah; and behold something greater than Jonah is here.

Luke 11:29-32

Overwhelmed but Not Overcome

Even through my stay at the hospital was brief I did observe that the environment varies or is dependent on the workers. Ultimately the attitude and policy of the administration is what controls the focus and the direction of a hospital. As one person has said water can only flow down a hill.

And as a patient you can tell a lot about the folks at the top by what is going on by their underlings at the bottom. A staff with a bad attitude can make you feel overwhelmed by the situation. Concurrently, if the staff has a good attitude it can translate as hopefulness to the patient. I believe it is the responsibility of the administration in any hospital to encourage their staff. They need to keep in mind that they are dealing with a whole person not just their physical body. This may account for the rise and popularity of holistic medicine.

Due to the fact that many of the workers have long hours, this often translates into indifference when care is given to the patient. I observed that often the emotional needs of the patient are either ignored or not acknowledged. This happens because there are often not enough competent workers and the staff is overworked and often exhausted. Given the fact that dialysis care is lengthy, patients are often very sick and needy both emotionally and physically. No wonder this procedure was sometimes less than perfect. I say this to offer an explanation in describing my next experience.

After my positive experience with a very competent Ken and Barbie, I wasn't terribly anxious about dialysis until something that made me realize that individuals can make all the difference in the world in hospital care especially when they are not as experienced or proficient in the area they are working in.

The process of dialysis can take anywhere from 2 ½ to 4 hours. For the time being I was being dialyzed every day. Sometimes the treatments were uneventful and sometimes they were horrendous. As I mentioned, the first couple of times, dialysis treatment was terrifying, but Ken, the male nurse stayed on top of my situation for the entire treatment. We discussed everything from theology to child rearing as he looked after me and several other patients. Thus my experience was a good one. But this was short lived.

On the third treatment Ken was gone and things went badly. A young short, and pudgy, Oriental nurse who I will call Sing Lee approached me. She seemed to have much less experience than Ken and Barbie. From the moment Sing Lee touched me everything was different, even the gauge of the needles she used. I am still not sure why she just didn't stick with the treatment procedure that Ken and Barbie had established. She decided to try something new and improved. I noticed she moved the knobs around *a lot!*

Later on, I jokingly suggested that perhaps she was checking my pain tolerance level. I'm not quite sure why she decided to change the amount of fluid withdrawn at the end but she did. This wouldn't ordinarily have been a problem except that she needed to check my particular record. In my case this was unnecessary because my kidneys were still removing fluid and I was extremely compliant with my diet because I was still being hospitalized.

As Sing Lee played with the dials my entire body went into spasms of incredible pain. I screamed in sheer agony writhing unable to relieve the pain that racked every muscle in my body. She wildly began adjusting the knobs. Then to her credit she rubbed and massaged my body so the charley horses would subside; even my chest area had gone into spasms. I had never experienced such pain.

Later, she admitted experimenting to see how much fluid she could take off forgetting that apparently that my kidneys had not entirely failed so I didn't need as much fluid removed. Why didn't she trust my chart? Why practice her medical skills on me? My muscles ached for days as though I had been competing in some Olympic type of race. I learned a hard lesson that day. One person can make all the difference in the world. It is years later and I still remember the agony of the experience vividly. Rick, my husband entered the room as I was being wheeled from dialysis.

"How are you doing," he asked in his usually chipper tone?

Too exhausted to speak, my color drained face revealed the ordeal that had occurred moments earlier.

"Was this what my new life held for me," a twisted thought suggested. "Now you're in for it and certain pain with every treatment, depending on the qualifications of the technician." It was a dismal prospect.

When Rick left my hospital room that night all I could do is weep. I opened my Bible to read and suddenly the strangest thing happen. I actually heard a sinister voice in my mind say.

"You're in my domain now and you will never survive the night. Your kidneys will fail and you will die then what will you do?"

Was this the voice of God warning me about impending doom of what was to come next? I had never felt such fear as I experienced that night. It was horrible, an immobilizing terror, making it impossible to complete the simplest task. This is the enemy of our souls, Satan, who often whispers to us in our weakest moment. Unable to move, I stared down at my lap and noticed my Bible open and read these familiar words.

> *Who is the man who fears the Lord? He (the Lord) will instruct him in the way he should choose. His soul will abide in prosperity, and his descendants will abide in prosperity, The secret of the Lord is for those who fear Him, and He will make them know*

His covenant. My eyes are continually toward the Lord, For He
will pluck my feet out of the net.

Psalm 25:12-15

As I read, I noticed that the fear of the Lord was different than that other
horrible, icy kind of fear. The fear of the Lord is being in awe and respect of
HIM. It was then that I figured out which fear was from God and which was
from the enemy of my soul, Satan. With God I felt instant comfort and peace.
I was so glad to be a Christian and continued to pray quietly. Then another
voice with incredible authority and peace flooded my mind and asked me the
following two things:

1)   who is the author of fear and,
2)   who is the one that disturbs you when you are reading your Bible?

Well, I knew that the author of fear was and still is… *the devil*. That
was a no brainer. I was learning quickly about the voice of God and the
voice of the enemy that can nag and keep your mind from a peaceful sleep.
I began to rebuke the devil and worship God. To my amazement the fear
left and a wonderful peace stayed. Then I read these amazing words from
my Bible.

> *Because he has loved Me I will deliver him, I will set him*
> *securely on high, because he has known my Name. He will call*
> *upon Me, and I will answer him: I will be with him in trouble;*
> *I will rescue him and honor him. With long life I will satisfy*
> *him, and let him know My salvation."*

Psalms 91:14-16

I put on my old friend Brother Rodney Howard-Browne and in the still
of the night I let the music and voice minister to my weary mind and soul.
Once again I felt a solace and divine peace for the next step of the journey.
Soon I drifted off to sleep. In what seemed like the middle of the night I heard
a deep and comforting familiar voice. It was my friend Dr. Jim Etheridge who
had just finished his evening rounds, coming to check on me. He was like an
angel. I stirred from my sleep.

Soon I was pouring out my heart. Jim listened patiently. All of my life I
shall always thank God for him because God used him to bring comfort to
me that night. He explained many things about what the tests result meant
and what I was going through.

God bless you, Jim for those healing hands and kind words! That evening God had showed me that He continually had me in the palm of His hand and that He had earthly and heavenly angels watching over me. I was indeed going to make it through.

> *He who dwells in the secret place of the most high, Will abide in the shadow of the Almighty. I will say to the Lord, "My refuge and my fortress, My God, in whom I trust!" For it is He who delivers you from the snare of the trapper, And from the deadly pestilence. He will cover you with his pinions, and under His wings you may seek refuge; His faithfulness is a shield and bulwark.*

> Psalm 91:1-4

Never-Ending Story

The worst thing about dialysis was the realization that it is like a never-ending story. Furthermore, the treatment as I explained earlier can vary from treatment to treatment. Many treatments can go awry particularly if the technician or nurse is either inexperienced or incompetent. In the next two years sadly I was at the mercy of both good and bad technicians. The preceding story was one of the many horrible things that I experienced.

I was beginning to understand why so many poor individuals went to such lengths to get a transplant while others would rather die than to endure the ordeal of unending treatments year in and year out. Perhaps this was why that doctor had decided that for me there really were no other options but to get a transplant.

The next morning I let Sing Lee know how much she had made me suffer. I like to think that it affected her but I don't know for sure if it did. She simply refused to look directly at me during the entire treatment. It was hard to relax during treatment knowing my life in her hands. If I was ever going to survive this ordeal I would have to know how to forgive and forgive and forgive.

Each day, in treatment, I needed God's grace. That is when God spoke to my heart, suggesting that I take the Rodney's music tape to the following day of treatment. When I did something happened that really rattled the staff. I was hooked up to the machine as usual and began listening to the tape. Suddenly, it was as if someone whispered in my head, "Get into your spirit man." I closed my eyes and thought, "How do I do that, God?" And it was as if God said, "I will show you."

I cannot relay how He showed me because I cannot articulate it with words but He did. Suddenly, I felt as though I was being lifted higher and higher. I saw clouds and then all these people in robes. It was wonderful. And oh the wonderful peace that overwhelmed me and surrounded me. I began laughing and laughing.

Somewhere, below me I could hear the voices and they were saying it must be a funny tape because the day before I had been screaming in terror.

God spoke to my spirit and said, "This is how the saints of old endured the lion's den, torture and burning at the stake but in America they do not need to have this revelation today because it is not necessary for their faith but you tasted just a little bit of it."

As wonderful as this was, I remember thinking, "I really would rather not have opportunity to really get further revelation along these lines." That was because I knew there had to be ongoing suffering. Suddenly the scripture came to mind.

> *For in the time of trouble he shall hide me in his pavilion: in the secret of his tabernacle shall he hide me; He shall set me up upon a rock. And now shall mine head be lifted up above my enemies round about me: therefore will I offer in his tabernacle sacrifices of joy; I will sing, yea, I will sing praises unto God.*
>
> Psalm 27:5

This was how I would face treatments day after day, by an amazing pattern of grace and divine intervention. Also, phone calls, letters and cards came from people just as I needed them as they felt impressed to send along a book or tape. They too, were my salvation. Sometimes friends from church would come over just to visit.

God was with me and soon what had been the dreaded hell on earth became routine and with God's help, faith began to conquer fear. As I look back it still amazes me the grace that God gave me during this incredible ordeal. But there were aspects that I treasure including a relationship with God that was far more precious than anything I had ever known or experienced. Truly, the scripture is accurate when it says.

> *"If we suffer with Him we will reign with Him."*
>
> Romans 1:17

Miracle Man

As I expressed earlier in the chapter, never in my life was I happier to have a personal relationship with Jesus Christ. I devoured the words from my Bible. They seemed to leap off the page and into my heart. I intuitively knew that I couldn't rely on some antiquated religious rhetoric or a religious *system* to get help.

I *knew* God would help me if I could just continue get to know Him personally. I was quickly learning to hear His wonderful voice and to distinguish Him from the voice of my own mind and other personalities like the voice of fear. The enemy of our soul is very real and definitely a challenge but not impossible to overcome with God's help. God promises through scripture indicated that I would get through this trial of my faith.

But often this thought would come into my mind, "If I had only lived in Bible times, then I could receive a miracle." Then the next thing I know a scripture would pop into my mind to correct my wrong thinking,

> *"Jesus the same yesterday, today and forever."*

> Hebrews 13:8

"So this is how the Holy Spirit speaks to our minds," I reasoned! This would be one of the most important keys to unlock the chain of fear; knowledge, understanding, reading my Bible and listening to His Spirit.

You cannot think two thoughts at the same time. Read about faith and it *will* displace fear. I began to study the Bible with a renewed fervor. Miracles occurred by the hands of Jesus in the New Testament when Jesus was alive, but could I get one by reading about them in my Bible? I reasoned that *if* the answer to that was yes, then that would mean I could get close enough to receive one! Day after day, I sought God and read my Bible.

> *"In the beginning was the Word and the Word was with God and the Word was God. And the Word became flesh and dwelt among us, (and we beheld His glory, the glory as of the only begotten of the Father,) full of grace and truth."*

> John 1:1 & 14

Jesus and the Word were one or equal.

To get to the Word was to touch Jesus. That was the answer I was looking for!

I also learned about Who the Holy Spirit was, and what He did in our lives. The Book of Acts states that, 'He *in us* is even more powerful than Jesus who walked the streets of Nazareth healing the blind and deaf two-thousand years ago.'

> *"But ye shall receive power, after that the Holy Ghost is come upon you: and ye shall be witnesses unto me both in Jerusalem and in all Judea, and in Samaria, and unto the uttermost part of the earth."*

Acts 1:8

Ultimately, God did let me reach my miracle as I sought Him with everything I had. The enemy did not steal my life from me because of my relationship with God. After all doesn't it say in the Bible that those who knew their God will do great exploits? I didn't know a lot about healing but this I did know. The biggest miracle had already occurred ... I was still alive!

All of my health challenges had been discovered in time for me to put up a good fight. I knew and had experienced enough about answered prayer to know that to beat this thing I must learn to pray effectively.

That is a vast difference from knowing *about* God to knowing God. I searched the Bible from cover to cover and found many wonderful truths. The truths I learned, is what this book is about. By reading this book you too can embark on your own miraculous journey.

> *In Him was life and the life was the light of men. And the light shines in darkness; and the darkness does not understand it. There was the true light which coming into the world enlightens every man.*

John 1:4, 5&9

> *He has blinded their eyes, and He has hardened their hearts; lest they see with their eyes and perceive with their hearts, and be converted, and I heal them.*

John 12:40

These passages suggest that by understanding and spiritual enlightenment from God's Word, your mind (and heart) can be activated. The extent to which the heart is affected or changed (or converted) according to God's word, is the extent to which health can be enjoyed by the physical body. I negotiated my way through the evil maze of confusion called sickness and received the miracle of a regenerated mind and body.

This is what the faith walk is really about. Read your Bible, and you will find that it is simply a collection of stories about the spiritual journey of ordinary people that battled seemingly insurmountable obstacles. But not only did they survive but they lived victoriously over the difficulties. God has always used weak and blemished vessels.

But was I too late? According to the doctor's, my kidney's were too far gone, for even God Himself to help. My greatest challenge would be to trust Him despite circumstances and doctor reports. As I pondered this information in my heart, I wondered. How would I know which direction to take?

Just then a nurse walked in with some rounds of medicines and to take my vital signs. All of a sudden she leaned towards me and added.

"I feel as though I need to give you a hug. This hug is from Jesus" she glowed with the love of God.

We both felt engulfed by a love much greater than mere human emotion can convey. It was divine. We basked in the glory of this divine visitation. When she finally left the room felt empty. I knew there and then that God would communicate and confirm the proper direction along the way, giving me the necessary confirmations when I needed it. I remember trying to read the directions to a recipe but not having a picture of the finished product. Then I turned a page and saw a picture of the finished product, I suddenly understood how to proceed. God was going to show me step by step the healing recipe and the finish product would be wholeness.

In summary, **first** we must realize that there is a vast difference from knowing *about* God intellectually than knowing and experiencing God *personally*. Look at it like this. I can know all about chocolate and may read every book written by chocolate experts, see a video on chocolates of the world. You can even interview chocolate experts *but* until you get up off your couch and go to the store and purchase the candy bar, you are still in the dark. You must personally taste the mouth watering dark chocolate with caramel and nuts in all its glory or **you are still clueless!**

Secondly, search your Bible from cover to cover for people that you can relate to that found themselves in equally difficult circumstances. Read the Bible as though God had personally written it for you. Put yourself in their places. Imagine the experience of actually being healed when you read about it in the scripture.

Thirdly, when you find an interesting truth or you are convicted that there is need for an adjustment in your life, write it down. When you get the chance go somewhere quietly and meditate on it and pray and ask God to work those truths into your life and change directions. If you are willing to do the difficult background work then God can do the miracle. Is it that simple? Yes! Eventually not only did I receive my healing but an experience and knowledge about God that will serve me for a lifetime.

Now are you ready to approach God? No matter how many mistakes you have made or how unworthy you feel, God has already taken care of those mistakes or sins as the Bible calls then through the sacrifice of His son Jesus Christ. By accepting Jesus as God's substitute as payment for *your* sins, **you can be forgiven**. This may appear to be overly simplistic but I assure you it is not.

According to *I John 2:12 and Romans 3:25, God put upon Jesus the wrath for our sins so that we don't have to bear the responsibility of them.* After your sin problem has been taken care of, you then can ask Jesus to come into your heart.

Pray this:

Father God, I come to you and ask that the Lord Jesus would please come into my heart. I know that I am a sinner. I thank you, Lord Jesus for coming and dying on a cross and redeeming me from my sin. I now accept and acknowledge You as my personal Savior and Lord. Fill me with your Holy Spirit that I may live for you while I am on this earth and please take me to heaven with you when I die. Amen!

Now that you have prayed this prayer often called 'the Sinner's Prayer' you have a personal relationship with God and His son Jesus Christ. By accepting the Lord and His sacrifice on the cross, you now can be filled with His precious Holy Spirit and therefore access all the promises mentioned in the Bible including healing. This is the beginning of your healing miracle and the most exciting journey of a lifetime. Are you ready to take the next step?

Chapter Review

1. **Jonah was willing to sacrifice himself for the sailors, who has paid the ultimate sacrifice for our sins?**

   _____

   _____

   _____

2. **If you have just prayed the 'Sinner's prayer' write down the date in the spaces below.   Now take a moment to quietly listen for any instructions you may receive from God and then write them down. If no message comes, simply continue to meditate on the chapter scriptures and then go on to the next chapter.**

_____

_____

_____

Chapter 7

Deep Blue Abyss

○ ○

Then Jonah prayed to the Lord, from the stomach of the fish, and he said, "I called out of my distress to the Lord, and He answered me. I cried for help from the depth of Sheol; Thou didst hear my voice." "For Thou hadst cast me into the deep, into the heart of the seas, and the current engulfed me. All thy breakers and billows passed over me. "So I said in myself, 'I have been expelled from Thy sight. Nevertheless I will look again toward thy holy temple. "Water encompassed me to the very soul, the great deep engulfed me; weeds were wrapped around my head. I descended to the roots of the mountains. The earth with its bars was around me forever," But Thou hast brought up my life from the pit, O Lord my God. While I was fainting away, I remembered the Lord and my prayer came to Thee, Into Thy Holy temple. "Those who regard vain idols forsake their faithfulness, but I will sacrifice to Thee with the voice of thanksgiving. That which I have vowed I will pay. Salvation is from the Lord." Then the Lord commanded the fish, and it vomited Jonah up onto the dry land.

Jonah 2:1-10

No Way Out

Plunged by a weary crew into this unique sepulcher, Jonah relentlessly sped towards a bottomless, opened mouthed black abyss. Imagine the prophet's hopeless descent of a lifetime. It must have seemed as if the motion had been delayed. Seized by the clutches of death, this poor man understood what horrors of death surrounded him. Churning currents like relentless jaws, clutched at Jonah's helpless form. The waves engulfed and carried him deeper and deeper towards his watery grave.

Terrifying thoughts possessed and tortured his frail human mind. Overwhelmed, by this tempestuous sea, Jonah must have tried to cry out in prayer only to have his bloated lungs fill with water.

Panic gripped his calloused heart and then struggle and finally resignation as Jonah completed the baptism of floodwaters immersing him into eternal damnation. After all he had disobeyed God and he knew that Sheol was the place prepared for rebellious mankind. Infraction of the rules was not to be tolerated. This was the just end declared by a righteous, supreme and Holy Deity for the disobedient prophet. Jonah instinctively knew he was getting what he deserved!

Religious and once upright Jonah, Prophet of the most High God understood that defiant actions met with dire consequences. Punishment, blackness, lost eternity was the judgment rendered for the wicked. Jonah understood what awaited him. There were *no* exceptions to these rules. He expected his punishment to be swift, terrible and complete with God as the jury, judge and executioner.

All that was left was for the sentence to be carried out. God must cleanse His own house first by punishing Jonah with the judgment he deserved! And that is why he had the sailors throw him overboard.

Jonah knew that evil, willfully disobedient, and vulgar heathens deserved punishment by God. Jonah had fervently preached this his entire life. Unfortunately he never imagined that *he* would one day become God's enemy in this strange turn of events. Nevertheless, now he must die for *he* had transgressed God's holy law. This he understood.

How had this ardent defender of justice, upholder of the law, this tin starred upstanding marshal of Jehovah turn renegade bandit? What else should be done now that he too had become wayward like so many of the evil nations about whom he prophesied? He let the sailors throw him over board because he didn't know of another system of justice. He did not know that a better covenant founded on grace, forgiveness and mercy was just around the corner.

Picture this scene in heaven. God folds His arms, taps his foot and waits impatiently all the while looking at his watch. "Wait, God I'm sorry, I've changed my mind, I'll go to Nineveh," Jonah cries out. Glug, glug, glug, Jonah sank quickly like some huge rock!

God had waited and watched as Jonah descended all the way down to the bottom of a sandy ocean floor. But before the prophet expired, God's booming voice cried out to a watching angel, "Stop the madness!" The angel swooped down and arranged a carrier to rescue the now repentant and soggy soul.

We are talking about one stubborn prophet. Consider what Jonah spoke of when he mentions the roots of mountains in verse six. We are familiar with the root system of a plant but where on earth are the roots of mountains? Jonah's foot had actually touched the ocean's floor. Every child that plays in the ocean knows that sandbars are ridges of sand made on the floor of the ocean by the sea currents.

Jonah literally hit bottom!

In the religion that Jonah preached and practiced there were no second chances. In other words there was no way for a repentant individual to be redeemed, especially if you were gentile. Jonah's system was simple, no deposit no return, in his case since he was Jewish and God appeared to have an affinity for Jews, it still meant three strikes and you're out. By the time, the angels had God take notice to looked over the case file carefully it was probably too late; by then it was more of an inquisition than a trial. Jonah preached a Gospel that had no leniency or compassion only judgment and condemnation.

The sentence was carried out swiftly. Even if Jonah did repent, there would be no possibly survival from this experience. He knew that God had been gracious in the past because he had experienced mercy but Jonah figured that he had probably exhausted God's mercy. But his situation was desperate and decided to give it one last cry; after all perhaps God wasn't counting.

Here is the amazing part, God not only intervened in Jonah's case but foreshadowed an aspect of grace that Jonah had never envisioned. In the twinkling of the eye and in one swift action, God upsets the applecart of Jonah's neat and systematic theology of an eye for an eye and a tooth for a tooth by giving Jonah another chance. God displayed more grace and forgiveness towards Jonah than he had ever imagined.

Our crusty Old Testament, hell fire and brimstone preacher is about to have another epiphany, but with a New Testament twist. He tastes the mercy of God in a fresh new way. Why? Because, God had a plan! God decided to use this incident with Jonah as a foreshadowing, or trial run of the patient character and amazing grace that will soon emerge on the pages of history in the form of His only begotten son Jesus Christ. Is this Almighty God practicing His pre-season batting and catching skills to one of His own home team players to see the reaction He can get? Perhaps!

Whiners, Gripers, Sinners & Saints

Jesus loves me this I know for the Bible tells me so. Do you remember that old Sunday school song? How does the Bible tell us so? By including stories that reveal how God's love is displayed toward His own wayward Jewish kids. Did God let Jonah have an amazing experience of being picked up by an enormous fish then deposited him on dry ground, simply to share with the folks back home? No! His life was spared to preach to the vilest heathens. That would be enough to end the story on a positive note but God had not finished with our main character yet.

Why did God use Jonah? Hidden in that question is the secret of the story. All can be summed up in one word mercy. Not man's mercy but the God kind of mercy. How else can you explain a book that features friendly cetaceans as heroes, rampaging hurricanes as the story backdrop and one rebellious preacher who turned savior for a bunch of pagans.

This was a script only God could write. One Jewish prophet sent on mission's trip to save not only himself, but the lives of pagan sailors and a city of idolaters who just happen to be savage enemies of Israel. Jonah watched God saving people that should have despised, rejected and destroyed. This is almost absurd as seeing Barney the purple dinosaur saving the city of Nineveh.

What better way to see the grace of God displayed on undeserving saints, sailors and sinners? Through this story we receive a sneak preview of the Messiah who will soon enter human history not as a center stage player but as a minor and insignificant baby born to a virgin. All of the Old Testament is an elaborate stage that introduces the world to a small Jewish nation Israel that produces a royal lineage that ultimately gives birth to the Messiah and Savior of the world Jesus Christ. Scripture tell us this man was meek and mild, hardly recognizable as royalty Who came not to be served but to serve. Not to Lord over but to yield, submit, surrender and eventually die for a lost humanity.

> *He shall not cry, nor lift up, nor cause his voice to be heard in the street. A bruised reed shall he not break and smoking flax shall He not quench: He shall bring forth judgment unto truth He shall not rail nor be discouraged till he has set judgment in the earth and the isles shall wait for his law.*

> Isaiah 42:2-3

In him we find a God who has always been less concerned with legalism and correct doctrine and more concerned with mercy, forgiveness and redemption. Mercy the personified character of Jesus Himself is center stage of the book called Jonah. That is why Jonah appears to be out of sync with the rest of the Old Testament prophetic books. In the middle of all these major and minor prophets judging nations, kings and kingdoms, we meet a backslidden minor prophet who delivers a message deflecting a major attitude change by God regarding gentiles. If there was ever a hope for this troubled world this is it.

A Red Rose for Ma

During my hospital stay more memorable adventures were right around the corner. One afternoon, Grace dropped by to see me after school bringing in the most beautiful bouquet including one of my favorite flowers, a beautiful red rose. Suddenly an impatient orderly disturbed our quiet room by hurriedly wheeling in an elderly female patient. Our peaceful tranquil room was transformed immediately into chaos as the old woman cut loose with the vilest train of expletives at the orderly that would have made Jonah's sailors blush. The attendant quickly exited leaving us alone with her.

We found ourselves staring across the room as a petite woman who returned a cautious glance. Grace and I grinned sheepishly at each other. Then Grace asked her a question, "I just bought this red rose for mom and its fragrance is so wonderful, would you like to smell it?"

I knew that Grace was doing her best to diffuse the charged situation and get the lady to relax but we were not prepared for what would happen next.

A small gruff and deep southern voice answered, "Of course, I've always loved roses, my husband likes to grow them and we have lots of citrus trees too."

And everyone just calls me, Ma." She added more gently, a smile creeping across a wrinkled prune like face.

Grace moved closer so Ma could get a whiff of the rose and then we asked if she minded our Christian music. She nodded eagerly, adding that she especially liked Southern Gospel music. We didn't have any but Grace went to work on that for the next visit.

After Ma was resting peacefully, I discreetly put on my glasses to get a closer look at my new inmate. Her countenance revealed a worn and hard expression. I surmised from her foul language and rough mannerisms that her lifestyle had been one of spiritual barrenness. I guessed my new roommate was in for a difficult time and I wasn't far from the mark.

Even though we crisscrossed between various procedures we were still able to pass some of those endless hours in that antiseptic hospital room talking. The more time I spent with Ma, the more I developed a compassion for this needy and colorful individual. Ma was from a family of circus performers.

I suppose that accounted for her hard life plus the unusual characters that streamed in daily to visit her.

Plus, Ma was never an easy patient to deal with. Whenever the doctors or technicians tried a procedure especially drawing blood, she would curse and scream at the doctors and nurses and then would pull out any apparatus they tried to hook to her arm. Exasperated, they would leave in a huff while I would try to calm her down saying,

"Now Ma, you know that they are only trying to help you."

She would nod her head in agreement and promise me that she would be more cooperative the next time but she never was. She was forever pulling out the needles or I.V. needles they put into her which made the most incredible mess on the floor.

The poor staff, unable to know what to do started strapping Ma in her bed. Lying helpless in her bed, her sad eyes reminded me of a wounded and caged animal. As I prayed silently for her, I came to realize that she was just like me, terrified and unsure of what tomorrow held. Then one night as I slept the strangest thing happened.

We both fell asleep or so I thought.

In the middle of the night I was hastily awakened by the feeling that someone staring down at me. I bolted upright in my bed as I felt someone's hot breath tickling my face. When I started to scream, I heard a familiar soft but gruff voice.

"Shhh, it's me, Ma," she said trying to reassure me.

"I just wanted to know what you looked like up close."

I tried to calm down my racing heart knowing there was no need to be terrified with this weak sickly woman or was there? It was then that I realized that Ma had more than just mere physical problems. She continued to stare down at me while I frantically pushed every button beside the bed, I could find. All the while I was speaking gently and reassuring to her.

"C'mon Ma, you know you ought to get back to bed. The staff is going to be pretty upset with you when they get here."

Meanwhile orderlies and nurses descended like a swat team racing around the corner and streamed into the room from every direction. They apprehended the ninety pound wayward sleepwalker and strapped her back in bed with a vengeance. That's when I noticed the stream of red blood trailing after her across the floor.

Loudly, I informed the orderly, "Look, there's a trail of blood coming from Ma."

In her eagerness to escape from bed, Ma had pulled out all the needles with the restraints that were attached to her again.

When I quickly pointed this oversight out to the orderly, he gave me an ominous warning and ordered me to never get out of bed without something on my feet. What did he mean by this? As if I needed more to worry about. Did Ma have some dangerous malady or blood disease that warranted this kind of precaution? Sleep was not about to be on the schedule that night because, no matter how many sheep I counted. As I stared blankly at the darkened hospital walls waiting for the sun to rise, my mind played the recording of the warning from the technicians,

"Whatever you do, don't get out of bed until this is wiped up and for heaven's sake make sure that you have something on your feet."

At that point I realized there was probably a lot about Ma that I didn't want to know. As we tried to fall asleep I spoke to Ma quietly.

"Are you still awake, Ma?"

"Yes," she responded more quietly.

"No one knew that you could even walk," I said carefully.

"Well …"she snarled and then added innocently,

"I can and there's a lot that they don't know about me. You been so kind to me and I just wanted to see what you looked like up close."

Still I was glad that Ma had no access to kitchen utensils. Ma was definitely a force to be reckoned with as the hospital staff found out.

Within minutes loud snores were coming from the bed across the room letting me know that Ma was fast asleep. Meanwhile I just stared up at the ceiling wondering what weird adventure lay in store for me next. The next morning I was more resolved than ever that I needed to go home.

I marched down the hall and waited for the doctor to come in for rounds. Coming around the corner his timid eyes met mine. I had guessed he was briefed on the night's antics. Giving him a hard stare, he quickly offered that I should be discharged the next day provided I had stabilized, seen the dietician and lined up dialysis treatment somewhere else in a nearby clinic.

Going back to my room I decided to tell Ma good news but she had already guessed what I was about to say. I approached Ma's bed cautiously as the watery blue eyes followed me. I saw her worried little face so I sat down next to her and took her small hand in mine. Then I put my tape player to her ear and a smile slowly moved across her face.

"You're leaving me aren't you?"

I said, "Yes, Ma," Do you know that Jesus loves you?"

She said matter of fact like, "Oh yes, of course, I know that, after all I used to go to be a member of the First Baptist Church!"

She had my attention. I had to admit that I was more than a little shocked. The thought quickly crossed my mind. How did a church person end up like this? Down the hall you could hear the orderlies bringing the breakfast trays so I moved back into my bed.

Breakfast was placed in front of her as had been done the day before but she hadn't touched it because she was strapped in again. I slipped out of my bed and over to Ma's, where her arms were tightly strapped by her side. There was no possible way for her to eat.

"Surely they will come and feed her," I thought, but no one ever came.

About forty-five minutes later I could hear the wheels of the orderlies with the food carts heading down the hall towards us to pick up our breakfast's trays.

Quickly I slipped out of my bed and over to her side and asked.

"Ma, would you like to eat?" she nodded yes vigorously.

I put my arm under her head to raise it a little, smoothed down the matted hair and fed her some mouthfuls of oatmeal very slowly. She was laboring to breathe a lot after each mouthful. She let me know that she was thirsty too, so I helped her take a few sips of water. After a couple of bites she closed her eyes and let me know that was enough. By then the orderly had arrived. Breakfast was swiftly taken away.

The orderly commented to Ma sharply,

"So, you've decided to take a bite or two."

I was angry at what I considered to be gross neglect but held my tongue and waited for the doctor's afternoon rounds. He would get a piece of my mind on the treatment of Ma. God was teaching me about compassion from both the patient's vantage point and the physicians. I knew that a patient with a bad reputation got poorly treated by all of the staff.

Finally, hours later, a young soft-spoken Indian doctor showed up. Naturally, Ma was ready to have him for breakfast pitching her usual cursing fit. He responded gently by trying to explain the necessity of the procedures. Her energetic mood swings always amazed me. My guess was that she saved up her energy for times like these. This time I did not sit idly by pretending not to listen. I was about to become a patient advocate. Carefully putting on bathrobe and slippers, I scrambled out of bed, and authoritatively held my hand up for everyone including Ma to hush. To my amazement they both did. Lack of articulation had never been a problem for me.

I began to articulate Ma's anger and frustration into pointed and careful language that the Indian doctor could understand. I also explained to him her fears and inability to fully comprehend what was going on because of the careless way she was treated. It bordered on gross neglect to tie her up and not have someone feed her.

Ma actually calmed down.

The doctor seemed relieved and commented, "I wish that I had known this earlier and I would have called you over sooner."

Then he added, "You are the best medicine for her. Ma is so much easier to deal with now that you are here."

I responded somewhat sarcastically to his comment,

"Sir, although I don't mind assisting you in this matter, I must remind you that I too am a patient and I am in for treatment, however if you wish to hire me for a salaried position when I get out I am more than happy to assist you."

He smiled, realizing by then, I was not serious.

Then I inquired, "Don't you have someone that can help this woman or give her some literature to help her understand what is going on?"

Sadly, he reminded me how understaffed the hospital was and as for the literature, there didn't appear to be any.

"Besides she wouldn't read it," he suggested.

He was probably right about that. That is when I began thinking about the book that I must write about all that I had seen and heard. To his credit the Indian doctor appeared to be compassionate and more conscientious than I originally gave him credit for. I believe some of my anger directed toward him was really my own frustration about my own situation and really had nothing to do with Ma at all. But I would learn more about this type of misdirected anger soon enough.

That same afternoon as I got all my appointments ready with the doctor and dietician and then packed my bag I noticed that Ma had been gone almost the whole day and that she was still missing in the evening when her family showed up. Every time I inquired after her, she was having another test. I thought that was a little unusual but didn't think anything more about it.

That night, Ma's family came in as usual, to visit her but Ma was still gone for yet another test. It was late and her earlier meals had never been touched. One of her sons came over to my bed and said in a soft southern accent.

"Ma'am may I speak to you?" he asked.

"Of course," I said.

He pulled his chair up besides my bed and told me that they so appreciated the love and kindness that I had shown Ma. They had admitted her to the hospital because she was having chest pains and breathing problems. That is when I found out Ma was a chronic alcoholic and chain smoker. She was in the process of drying out which is why her behavior was so erratic.

I knew that sometimes her family gave her cigarettes and wheeled her outside for a smoke even though it was forbidden, but after all that was their business.

"Today the doctor told us that the test results have revealed that Ma has an aggressive cancer condition." He continued the story while I considered it all.

Ma didn't have long to live and he wanted me to know that. When this grown son began to weep so did I. Ma's husband who had been watching us moved over towards me and opened up his wallet to reveal a picture of a beautiful shapely and immaculate woman with long dark hair

"This is what she looked like when I married her, she was so pretty," he blew his nose into a large red checkered handkerchief.

I had to agree. Ma had been a beautiful woman.

Once again the night came. This time I was awakened by screaming. The nurses came quickly running down the hall but to my surprise they did not come in. They only shut the door, leaving me inside with Ma screaming. I got out of my bed to calm her down but it didn't seem to help. I ran down the hall corridor to the nurse's station and said if something wasn't done I would call the doctor myself.

It was then that I realized Ma's problem wasn't only physical but physiological as well. Since the hospital staff is equipped to deal with physical symptoms, they simple ignore the deeper spiritual and emotional needs of the patients.

Unfortunately, like snipping a weed growing beside a plant, when the root of the problem is not dealt with, the weed will continue to grow again until it finally chokes out the plant. In Ma's case the problem was much deeper than just physical. When you know right from wrong and choose the wrong your conscience is always there to let you know that you made the wrong choice. And all the alcohol in the world can never numb the pain and realization of knowing your life could have been so much more. It was obvious to me that Ma was a woman sick in body, mind and spirit.

The next day I was released from the hospital but before leaving I walked one last time over to Ma's bedside to look into those tired and sad eyes. It felt as though I could almost see into her tormented and wounded soul. Not knowing what else to do, I plugged in the ear phones and put them into her ears and then put the player cassette into her wrinkled hands and placed one of my red roses on her bed.

"This is for me?" she asked as one lone tear trickled down the wrinkled cheek.

"Yes, Ma," I said,

"Just remember the words of Jesus before he left his disciples to go to heaven. Lo, I am with you always even to the end of the world. Ma, Jesus will never leave you or forsake you." Brushing a tear of my own away, I prayed for Ma one last time and left the hospital room.

An amazing realization came over me that day. The Good Shepherd really did keep track of His sheep and was bringing this one lost lamb back to the fold. Although, I never had the opportunity to see Ma again in this life, I hope to see her in the next.

> *"The Lord is my Shepherd; I shall not want. Even though I walk through the valley of the shadow of death, I will fear no evil for thou art with me;"*

Psalm 23:1& 4

Chapter Review

1. **Give a brief summary of what Jonah said in the belly of the whale?**

   _____

   _____

   _____

2. **What example in this chapter let's us know that God does keep track of his sheep?**

   _____

   _____

   _____

Front row: Andy, Joy, Eileen
Back row,: Rick & Pete

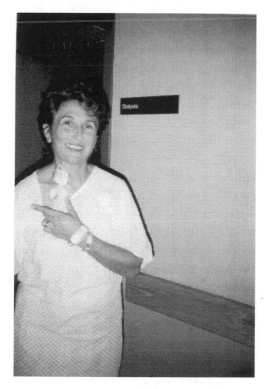

Eileen

Eileen, Darlene, Leilani

Front row: Joy, Andy, Eileen Grace
Back row: Rick, Pete, Dave

Eileen & Rick

Chapter 8

Say It Again Jonah

○ ○

Now the word of the Lord came to Jonah the second time, saying, "Arise, go to Nineveh the great city and proclaim to it the proclamation which I am going to tell you." So Jonah arose and went to Nineveh according to the word of the Lord. Now Nineveh was an exceedingly great city, a three days walk. Then Jonah began to go through the city one day's walk; and he cried out and said, "Yet forty days and Nineveh will be overthrown."

Jonah 3: 1-4

God of the Second Chance

After that amazing experience we imagine old Jonah attired in a fleecy bathrobe and bedroom slippers seated in his favorite lazy boy recliner eating some of mom's favorite lentil soup. Out of the blue, that old familiar voice comes to Jonah.

"Jonah, **Jonah,** **Jonah!!!"**
Meekly, Jonah responds, **"Yes, Lord."**

God says, "Go to Nineveh!" Never in a million years had Jonah imagined that he would get a second chance. Oh to have been a fly on the wall during that session with God! Like a World War II destroyer that takes a direct hit from the enemy sub and then is asked to go out again, Jonah must have cringed at the thought. We will never know what transpired other than the fact, that when he was asked to complete this dangerous assignment behind enemy lines, he agreed to go.

Oh the butterflies, oh the queasy stomach but Jonah knew this time he had better not chicken out! In the annals of Bible history, Jonah was not the *only* reluctant prophet that is asked more than once to finish the job. Many times these men of God confronted formidable odds. For example the young prophet, Jeremiah had a very difficult charge that God warns him about.

> *"Because everywhere I send you, you shall go, and all that I command you, you shall speak. Do not be afraid of them "Now gird up your loins, and arise, and speak to them all which I command you. Do not be dismayed before them, lest I be dismay you before them."*

Jeremiah 1:7, 8 & 17

Did this prophet have a similar 'spiritual' hearing problem like Jonah? What has to amaze the average reader of this scripture is the patience that God displays in dealing with His servants. He doesn't zap them but instead gives them a second chance even when an individual like Jonah has blatantly disobeyed Him. It is obvious that God understands humans and their 'fear of man' flaw handed down from great, great grandpa Adam, who fell in the garden because of peer pressure from Eve.

Clearly, God's agenda is always multi-faceted. In defense of Jonah and prophetic peers, we must remember that they were ordinary men appointed by God for an extraordinary task. Why was Nineveh a challenging assignment? Again looking to scripture for further understanding we find an interesting passage from book of Nahum that appears to shed light on the subject.

> *Woe to the bloody city, (Nineveh) completely full of lies and pillage; her prey never departs. The noise of the whip, the noise of the rattling of the wheel, galloping horses, and bounding chariots! Many slain a mass of corpses, and countless dead bodies. They stumble over the dead bodies! All because of the many harlotries of the harlot, the charming one, the mistress of sorceries, who sells nations by her sorceries.*

Nahum 3:1

Historically, this passage seems to reinforce what we already know about these people. Nineveh, located on the Tigris River was settled by the fierce Assyrians famous for having one of the largest and most splendid cities as well as barbaric. In modern times it is located on the opposite side of the modern city of Mosul in Iraq. It is recorded to be founded by Nimrod, the son of Ham, in Genesis10: 9-11.

With more than 22,000 inscribed clay tablets, their scholars leave records that inform us of not only their own accounts of creation and the flood but furnish us with invaluable background records that complement our own understanding of Old Testament information.

These records are also replete with descriptions of beautified royal palaces, libraries and a modern water system of aqueducts. Although the actual city was probably only three miles in length it also had suburbs that were considered part of the city much as the burrows are considered part of New York City.

This may also explains why, some historians, record Nineveh as being about 60 miles in circumference and why Jonah took more than three days to cover the entire city and its surroundings suburbs.

Many times a particular message given by God revealed His will for nations that the prophet served. This particular job assignment was perceived as more difficult because it departed from the normal job description for Jonah because he had to confront a hostile enemy of Israel. It wasn't that Jonah wasn't used to foretelling impending judgment on various cities, and kings but he was accustomed to speaking to Israel. Given that these men tended to live simple lifestyles in monastic type like cloisters, it is understandable that this interpreter for God would balk at an assignment of this magnitude to a hostile audience.

We must also remember that given the explosive tendency of these old sovereigns who behaved like tyrants, it is understandable that it was with great apprehension, dread and fear for their lives that the prophetic messengers confronted these wealthy, sinful and spoiled despots! But Jonah puts on his favorite pair of Adidas sneakers and began heading eastward toward the desert region before Nineveh. Arriving at the fair city he began to preach. Despite Jonah's initial hesitancy and reluctance, the tables turn so completely that by the end of his first day walking, he not only has the attention of the city but royal curriers have informed their king of Jonah's presence.

Is it the words that wax eloquent coming from Jonah lips that convinces the city to amend its wicked ways or is it something else that grabs their attention? And how is it that the fearsome Ninevites including their king became intimidated enough by their unusual guest to the point that the sovereign issues a decree for all the people to follow?

Chocolate, Nuts and Denial

Helen the dietitian at the dialysis center explained to me about the whys and wherefores of my new diet. Kidneys are responsible for many things including the removal of wastes and fluid from the body. They also make red blood cells as well as regulate body chemistry including blood pressure. Consequently, I not only needed to monitor all fluids but I also needed to watch various minerals since my body was not able to get rid of numerous unnecessary elements. If these nutrients were too prevalent in my system they could do a great deal of damage.

If particular potassium, phosphorus, sodium or protein deposits built up, they were particularly dangerous. Therefore, I had to become familiar with things that contained large amounts of these nutrients. Sodium would cause me to hold water, phosphorus would make my bones weak and body itch while potassium would cause my heart to stop or beat irregularly while extra protein deposits would make something else in my body malfunction. None of these things filled me with happy thoughts.

I also had to watch my fluid with things that I never even considered as fluid such as ice cream, gravy and soups. As time went on my body could filter out less and less water. Retaining water is the most uncomfortable thing that can happen because the excess fluid finds its way into your lungs which can fill up with fluid and prevent you from breathing. So, the process of weeding out my favorite foods began. No more pizza, spaghetti sauce, no beans, no condiments of any kind, not too much meat and of course no cheese and milk products, no coffee, limited tea, no chocolate of any kind including of course no Hershey's candy bars and on and on the list went. That would be enough to make any one depressed.

No kind of chips or, colas, nuts, coconuts, yeast or wheat germ. Limited fruits and definitely no melons, bananas, date, figs, or dry fruits or even oranges or grapefruit. Limited vegetables, no baked potatoes, no canned foods that contained salt, and no frozen prepared goods because of the salt.

I remember asking her, "Was there any food left? What could I eat?"

No wonder I lost twenty pounds in no time. I always wanted to be nice and thin but now it was no longer associated with the joy as I imagined it would be. On the positive side, I could fit into all of 17 year old Grace's jeans. Being from a middle-eastern culture, I never realized how much emotional satisfaction and joy I derived from eating my favorite foods, now that so many things were denied, I had to find pleasure in other things like sniffing.

As difficult as it was for me, we decided that Friday night would still be our Pizza night even though the most I could hope for was to sniff the pizza and maybe chew on the left over end of a piece of hard crust. I did become very good at sniffing things for enjoyment. Pretty pathetic but true! Can you imagine my family trying to enjoy a meal knowing that mother would be watching and sniffing? We had to come up with a strategy to keep the kids from feeling guilty.

Unknowingly my sister and brother-in-law came up with a brilliant reverse psychology for handling this. Rather than allow me to feel sorry for myself, my sister who enjoys good chocolate found out that there was a Fanny May chocolate store in Tampa.

She decided to get several boxes so that she could, "Share it with the kids," or so she said!

When she and brother-in-law Keith returned from the candy store they brought out the four boxes of chocolate, opened them up and then placed them in the middle of the kitchen table. Then the craziness began. All of them, except me of course began to sample the delectable treats! It was a chocoholic feeding frenzy. It had been a while since everyone including the children had had any chocolate because of my severe dietary restrictions.

So they began digging into those mouth-watering chocolates and promptly gorged themselves, everyone that is, except me. Our house was filled with peals of laughter as these greedy modern day Hansel and Gretel children bit into mouthfuls of that dark and milk chewy chocolate stuff or caramel pecan and oh those heavenly gooey raison filled white things with peanuts.

"Ooh this one has toffee bits with macadamia nuts or that one has chocolate with peanut butter cream filling," Keith teased. Before we knew it the kids and even Rick had picked up on the fun and began to copy Uncle Keith's antics, knowing full well I couldn't eat any of this.

Suddenly the doorbell rang and everyone stopped in their tracks. Our good friend Dr. Jim Etheridge had just decided to drop over the house to see how I was doing. He was truly horrified at the cruelty of this three-ring circus of chocolate binging and could not find humor in any of it.

"Isn't it enough that your mom can't eat any of this stuff without parading it all in front of her that way," Jim demanded as compassionately for my sake as he could?

"We're just kidding," my guilty family responded.

"Seemed more like tormenting than teasing to me," Jim responded. But in the end, it was the right thing to do.

My sister and brother-in-law had actually chosen to give my children an important object lesson. Why should the children have unnecessary guilt and be further burdened and messed up by being denied special goodies and treats like chocolate? Wasn't the family suffering enough? Unnecessary denial of the fun foods in their life because of their mother's sickness was wrong. Life with a sick mom was hardship enough.

My daughter Joy said that she never did get over feeling guilty! She has always been extremely sensitive to the pain of others. A mom unable to eat food at restaurants or even at times unable to attend school events was always difficult for her. The children needed to indulge in some simple pleasures even if it had to be done in front of mom. Life was going on and it was still O.K to laugh and have fun. My sister Leilani and her husband Keith knew my children couldn't stop living because of mom's sickness.

Mom wouldn't break and life didn't revolve around her needs. Also, they weren't going to permit me to feel sorry for myself for long. Mom was not going to be allowed to be some Prima Donna to be waited on hand and foot.

As you can imagine our whole family looked forward to the joy and surprises that my sister and brother-in-law brought with them as they traveled to and from Tampa each and every weekend without fail. They often made it a point to take the children and Rick to eat knowing this was now such a special treat. They also helped to clean the house or do whatever else was necessary to help our family. Their commitment to me never wavered in this ordeal.

Without a doubt it was one of the most special times with all of our family and I don't know what we would have done without Leilani and Keith. I will never forget their great love and sacrifice and in the end it was this sister who stepped forward to donate her kidney to me. I will always be thankful that my family did not allow me to pity myself or use the sickness as a guilt trip to control the family's eating habits as so many people do but more about that later.

Saying goodbye to fast food places with Mexican, Chinese, Italian, burgers and salty fries as well as the Colonel's fried chicken and that famous bloomin' onion was no easy task. Actually some of these places I really didn't miss but it was just the idea that I couldn't eat there that made it so tough.

As time passed I started to go out to restaurants and when I did the family looked extra hard at the food as if it was a great adventure. Everyone made a game out of it, trying to figure out what on the menu I could eat without getting sick. One time we went to Olive Garden and having to look past lasagna and Alfredo dishes was torturous.

"Hey Mom, I bet you can eat a plain salad or what about a vegetarian dish?" the children would suggest.

"Yum, yum, I can hardly wait," I offered sarcastically.

I remember one time when my daughter Grace and her two friends, Leslie and Andrew were over for dinner. We did the pizza delivery thing. Without missing a beat, I sat down and sniffed the various kinds of pizza for enjoyment. We never thought it was strange until Andrew pulled Grace aside later and quietly remarked,

"Why doesn't your mom eat with everyone? I never heard of anyone just sniffing dinner," Andrew quizzed Grace.

So Grace explained to him my dietary limitations.

The moral to the story is this. Sick people can become so self-absorbed, they forget about those precious family members that are suffering right along besides them. During a health crisis, family members need to come up with positive strategies especially related to those difficult issues of prolonged health challenges.

Feel free to use our family's "in your face" creative ideas.

Doris Day and Religion March On

As I said earlier sometimes it was easier to stay home than attend a function with my husband that included a meal. I remember going to a wedding and passing up the prime rib and cheesecake. The staff at the dialysis clinic advised me to make up the calories by eating all the sugary stuff I wanted like Jello, cool whip, hard candy or sugar or salt free canned vegetables and canned fruit.

"No thank you." I argued and added.

"With that type of diet being so nutritionally deficit it would only be a matter of time before I would get sicker or develop some other type of disease."

I opted to take my chances and limit the amount of fresh fruits and vegetables but for nutrition sake, kept as many fresh and vitamin filled foods in my diet as possible.

Another thing that confused and frustrated me was that although the staff knew the dangers associated with the food we ate, I felt as though the dialysis staff actually sabotaged the patient's health by allowing them to order food that was very unhealthy for them during treatment. One staff member said that *it all comes out* during the dialysis but what about the other organs that would be affected like the heart or arteries? And what was that meeting with Helen for???!!!!

Foods like fried chicken, sausage biscuits and cheesecake that are supposed to be definite no no's and yet patients were allowed to eat these things all the time during treatments. It was a confusing message to say the least. The staff appeared to have a Doris Day approach. Whatever will be will be. The future's not ours to see etc. It was an approach that I could not condone.

To me it was like having your kids *only* eat candy and desert constantly. Why not stress nutrition and exercise and keep patients as disciplined and fit as possible without treating us as spoiled children to be indulged?

Naturally, I guarded what I ate with a religious fervency because *I believed* I would get better. Some patients had no faith and nothing to hope for. This was the greatest tragedy. Meanwhile, I watched in horror as the patient's indulged and ordered out for any and every type of harmful food imaginable *during* their dialysis treatment while the staff appeared to look on indifferently.

I realized that the staff did this partly due to the fact that the patients *did indeed* act like children and partly due to the fact that many of the patients were not likely to improve. They reasoned that since most of the patients would not survive long on the treatment; why not let them enjoy themselves with trivial pleasures.

To me it was like ordering the last meal for a condemned prisoner.

Between painful treatments every other day, subsequent exhaustion after the treatments and numerous physical limitations including diet, it is easy to understand why ongoing depression is an immense hurdle for the dialysis patient. Is it any wonder that patients often felt sorry for themselves? Added to that hopeless environment, sprinkle in a few grains of a placating staff willing to pamper the patients at any cost with all types of "illegal "food.

Had God Forgotten Me

As I approached my first Thanksgiving on such a restricted diet, I sought God with everything I knew. I began to fast for some more answers. Maybe God needed more time than I had originally anticipated. Or perhaps it would take forty days, after all that was the time of testing of the Israelites in the desert and didn't it rain 40 days and nights for Noah and the animals on the arc? Of course 40 days came and went. Then, I thought it must be that God's will take 120 days to heal me. After all the disciples waited 120 days in the upper room for the Holy Spirit. Then 120 days came and went. No matter how many times I worked out the time frame for this trial, the days came and went and I still was on treatment. Then the reality check came. Maybe God had forgotten me.

Meanwhile at the dialysis sanitary treatment plant, as I referred to it sarcastically, I was ordering weekly tests to *confirm the miracle* that I knew God was going to do any day now. Every week the tests revealed no change. Yet I was still determined that "my" manifested miracle would arrive any day. I'm ashamed to say that I verbally witnessed to the doctors, the nurses, the techs, the patients even floor sweeper, and anyone that breathed. Any day my miracle would happen. Poor Dr. Serrano was so kind and patient with me but informed me that the weekly tests must end, as he could not justify them to the insurance company.

Finally Thanksgiving came and went and Christmas holidays began to approach. I never felt so desperate in my life. Would God allow my faith to be ridiculed by enduring another holiday? The staff put up a tiny and gaudy aluminum tree with red balls as the dialysis patients prepared themselves for the holidays. The sad reality being, that there are no holidays or days off for the sick.

Various patients began to bring in little goodies for the staff. Naturally they involved the "contraband" foodstuff that we were not supposed to have. How could they be thankful for a staff that inflicted so much pain on us? In truth, they were better witnesses to faith because they did not witness with their lips but with their actions like I should have.

After all, actions do speak louder than words. I certainly had a lot to learn but all I felt was tremendous resentment and anger towards the staff. Why? I'm ashamed to say this but I could not separate them from the ordeal I was going through plus I didn't want to get too comfortable.

Any day now I would be out of there so I stayed aloof from everyone. It reminded me of the time years earlier when several of us from the local church went to the prison to witness. Without exception, all of the inmates said that they were innocent and that their lawyer would have them out any day now. Of course we all knew differently. "Are they kidding?" I smirked to my friends everyone knew that 99.9% of them were guilty as sin. So too the dialysis nurses and doctors thought I was nuts and in denial of my sickness.

I began to doubt myself. Things looked pretty bleak. I fought depression and couldn't understand why God wasn't answering my prayers. I knew He could but maybe He didn't want to. Perhaps it was because I wasn't someone important like a preacher or president. Or maybe I didn't have what it took in terms of not enough faith. Perhaps God was unwilling because I was unlovely as the reflection that I saw in the eyes of some of the nurses that took care of me. If that was true then I guess I didn't deserve to be healed.

What I didn't know then, but know now is that He *was* answering each and every prayer but *His* priority of answered prayer was different. I had counted the hours then the days and weeks but finally, the weeks turned to months and finally months into years. God was answering a higher prayer than even I understood.

He was busy bringing people and situations in my path to change bad attitudes and patterns of thinking. God wanted to heal *my soul* before He healed my body!

In dialysis you must go on the shift that is not full. They switched me around to accommodate my work schedule and sometimes that meant the late shift. Often times I got home at night and my little eight year old son Andy was in bed asleep or my daughter, Joy in Jr. High was heading off to take a shower. It broke my heart that I was no longer home in the evenings for supper with my family or to help children with school work but if you really want to know the proverbial straw that broke the camels back. Read on!

Since all of these health challenges occurred during the first week of classes and I had a full load no one was really sure if I would be able to return to work. Against the wishes of my good friend and physician Dr. Serrano I returned to work as soon as I got out of the hospital. I wanted to finish the semester that I had begun. As impossible as it sounds despite all the incredible circumstances I returned to work by the third week. As I said earlier, I was very, very determined.

Naturally, everyone at the university was shocked to see me back never mind me returning to my full load. I had lost twenty pounds and I was not very heavy to begin with. My clothes hug on me like a scarecrow but I was not going to let this thing lick me. I taught classes before and after treatment.

Plus, I never even let my classes know what was going on. I would begin standing and finish my lectures seated with the overhead machine nearby. Occasionally, a student would come up to me and ask if I was all right. I would always nod in the affirmative but my sallow colored skin was a giveaway, that all was not alright. Did I mention that I was determined and stubborn with an inner resolve that was hard to explain? Each day I would pray and ask the Holy Spirit to give me the strength to go on but what God had to rid me of was being *too hard headed*!

Determined or Hard-Headed

Dr. Jimmy Duplass, a colleague, had shared that the evening class had been given the choice to go to another professor but had refused. That made me even more determined to finish. I just couldn't let them down. They had put their confidence in me. I had to finish what I started.

I remember watching a film about General Patton in World War II rescuing a group of American soldiers that were surrounded by Germans. With low rations, and snow falling, the outnumbered camp was enclosed and pounded by the enemy fire repeatedly and yet refused to give up. The enemy in one final attempt raised the white flag of surrender and came into the tiny camp offering them one last chance to surrender. Undaunted by circumstances they responded and returned the note. Scrawled across the message was simply the word, "Nuts."

The Germans really didn't fully understand the colloquialism but somehow understood these tenacious American soldiers were not about to quit. When General Patton found out about the response given by the surrounded American army, he remarked to his staff that these guys just had to be rescued. The General in his usual sarcastic form put it this way, "Anyone that articulate deserves to be saved."

And of course they were.

Was God looking at me to see if I was tenacious enough to continue to believe despite my circumstances? Against all odds, would God, like General Patton determine to rescue one that would not entertain defeat? I hoped so!

Moreover, if the class were canceled some of these students would be delayed in their program or perhaps not graduate. I couldn't let that happen. What an incredible challenge. Could I really do it? Although, I felt weak, I continued on. Week after week, class after class, I pressed on determined to finish what I started. The class never knew I was on dialysis only that I had been hospitalized. I was a professional and was committed to finishing and I did. The last day of class I talked to them about commitment. Commitment to finish what you started; the class got very emotional. Tears were in some of their eyes. I never revealed the specifics of what I was struggling with but it didn't matter they got the idea. Plus I didn't want to distract them from the real message. When you are committed to something, you finish, no matter what! You could have heard a pin drop. When you speak out of your heart and soul, it has a reverberating ring of truth that distinguishes it from mere intellectual knowledge. I often tell my students that more things are caught then taught and they caught something big that night!

During this time, I had many incredible experiences that are indelibly etched in my mind. Some were positive and some definitely were not. Like the time I was rushing to my night class right after dialysis. I remember picking up my heavy book bag with the arm that had been used as the site for the needles to enter. I was warned repeatedly by the attending nurse John to please slow down and not rush to class. The holes in my arms where the needles went in needed to be completely clotted off before rushing off to teach but I was very stubborn. "

"Slow down Eileen," John urged.

"Yah, Yah, John you're worse than my mother," I called back over my shoulder.

This was one of those times when being hard headed did not pay off.

My sites where I had been dialyzed had not clotted enough. When I grabbed the heavy book bag, blood began to spurt everywhere from the weight of the textbooks inside. Like a great oil gusher, blood spurted everywhere. Blood went on the floor, the furniture, all over my white blouse that I had to go to work in. Not only did it shake me up but I felt bad because of the mess that my carelessness had caused John. As he patiently mopped up the mess he looked up at me and once again encouraged me to pah-lease slow down a little. This time I was listening. I thought that as a Christian I was supposed to be above circumstances like this. Once again this simple routine and attending to details in the world of dialysis, further reminded me that I was not as invincible as I once thought.

Did you know that that there is a fine line between resolve, determination, tenacity and all those other good traits and stupidity, stubbornness and being hard-headed? It is great wisdom when one knows the difference between the two. I was about to learn the difference of when to stick to my guns and when to listen to advice of others.

In one of the earlier dialysis shifts, I was in with a group of people that were from the inner city. They came to dialysis in a van. Of course with my superior intellectual and spiritual attitude, I refused to speak to or connect with anyone until something happened one day that changed all of that.

A good Christian is *supposed* to witness and to pray for them and I did make sure to fulfill my religious obligation. But when I was finished I would turn my earphones on, listening only to praise and worship or Bible tapes. After all what knowledge could they possible possess that could interest or relate to my life?

Sad to say I was religiously sickening. Bible verses would fall profusely from my untainted and pure lips. And I was determined not to associate with any riff raff. What a bad witness I was! I was never agreeable but always demanding and difficult, insisting on my own way, refusing to comply to even the simplest request of a staff person.

I would dismiss them saying this is not a good time. I refused this or that procedure on principle, refused to fill out paperwork if I could possibly get out of it. How clever I was in those days. Secretly, I knew that all they really wanted was to assert control over my life, never realizing that control was really *my* issue.

God was about to set my course in a direction that I neither planned for nor wanted. I was about to sail into some of the greatest challenges and receive some of the hardest knocks yet. Along the way, God would arrange for me to meet some of the saintliest people this side of heaven, and in the process receive an important attitude adjustment.

Chapter Review

1. **What does Jonah decide to do when God gives him a second chance?**

   _____

   _____

   _____

2. **What is the difference between being determined and being stubborn?**

   _____

   _____

   _____

Chapter 9

How to Cancel Calamity
& Delete Disaster

○ ○

Then the people of Nineveh believed in God; and they called a fast and put on sackcloth from the greatest to the least of them. When the word reached the king of Nineveh, he arose from his throne, laid aside his robe from him, covered himself with sackcloth, and sat on the ashes. And he issued a proclamation and it said, "In Nineveh by decree of the king and his nobles: do not let man, beast, herd, or flocks taste a thing. Do not let them eat or drink water. But both man and beast must be covered with sackcloth; and let men call on God earnestly that each may turn from his wicked way and from the violence which is in his hands. Who knows, God may turn and relent, and withdraw His burning anger so that we will not perish?" When God saw their deeds, and that they turned from their wicked ways, then God relented concerning the calamity that He had declared He would bring upon them. And He did not do it.

Jonah 3:6-10

Special Delivery

Was it merely the man's words that waxed so eloquent or was it the appearance of God's special delivery person. Could the babblings of a simple itinerant preacher be sufficient to warrant the attention of an entire city? No one can say for sure. What we do know is that there was something special about *this* particular prophet that grabbed the Ninevites attention. From the lowest citizen to the highest official, even the king repented.

Perhaps a bleached 'ghostly' prophet walking around would have the ability to both convict and scare the Ninevites into repentance. Searching the web and other resources for incites on the Old Testament passage revealed some remarkable and startling information!

Over the years there have been some interesting factual recordings about men who have been swallowed by whales or other large fishes. What captivated me most was a story recorded in the book, *Sixty-three Years of Engineering*, written by Sir Frances Fox, The story went something like this.

"In February, 1891, the whale-ship, *Star of the East*, was in the vicinity of the Falkland Islands, when a lookout sighted a large sperm whale three miles away. "Suddenly, one of the harpooning boats was upset by the strong lash of a whale's tale. One of the men involved was drowned, while the other man, James Bartley, simply disappeared and was presumed dead."

When the whale was killed, the sailors worked frantically all day and night, as was their habit, to dissect the fish. As they worked on the whale's stomach, they were startled by "spasmodic signs of life coming from inside." To their utter amazement and shock, they found the missing sailor, doubled up and unconscious. He was then laid on the deck and treated to a bath of sea water which soon revived him but his mind was still not clear. He was placed in the captain's quarters where he remained a "raving lunatic."

At the end of the third week the sailor had entirely recovered from shock and resumed his duties. Now we come to the reason for including this excerpt and what I think is the highlight of his adventure.

"During his sojourn in the sperm whale stomach, Bartley's skin was exposed to the action of the gastric juices, and thus underwent a striking change. His face, neck and hands were bleached to a deadly whiteness, and took on the appearance of parchment."

Bartley affirms that he would have lived inside his house of flesh until he starved. He lost his senses through fright but not from lack of air.

"Was this what happened to Jonah," I thought to myself?

Bartley further went on to explain that after he fell into the foaming waters from the lashing of the whale's tail, "he was drawn along into the darkness where the heat was intense. As he tried to find a way out and touched the slimy walls all around him, he suddenly realized where he was and the shock produced the unconscious state in which he was found."

This account would seem to lay aside the debate that scholars have had for centuries regarding the authenticity of the Jonah's tale regarding whether or not an individual could actually survive such an ordeal. There can be no doubt that it was possible. It was not even difficult to find several accounts of similar incidents. The important information here is the testimony given by the sailor himself about his reaction in the whale belly and the latter strange appearance or 'bleached to deadly whiteness,' afterwards.

If the Ninevites saw someone walking around in their city with a ghostly appearance they just might take notice. They may have wondered, "Is he real or merely some strange apparition from beyond the grave?"

Then add to that one raving and babbling old prophet, "Yet forty days and Nineveh will be overthrown" That might have been enough to win them over.

Nineveh-Fruits of Repentance

So these worldly Assyrians listened intently, and then acted. If only Christians would respond that quickly. The Ninevites were one of the most feared people groups in all of the Old Testament. Yet in front of them stood a unique object lesson created by God Himself! They might have repented en masse so they wouldn't end up like him.

Imagine the local television station having a live and exclusive interview for the six o'clock news with none other than the Prophet Jonah himself. Jonah's style of, in your face preaching would have had them on the edge of their seats.

Then perhaps they would cut to the local roving reporter down in the street to interview the toothless old market lady, who first spotted what she thought was the ghost of Christmas past, entering the city gate early Monday morning as she was getting ready to set up her onions and garlic. Then, Mohammed, the crossed eyed unscrupulous camel salesman that everyone knows, waves his hands in terror and tells the king's regent about how serious this is. Like today's modern prophets of gloom and doom, they were convinced this *had* to be the end of the world! When everyone finally saw that even the king was terrified enough to get on sack cloth and ashes, surely the situation was *that* perilous.

Finally the man of the hour, Jonah himself, appeared with skin whiter than death itself with pierce black bulging eyes, furiously wagging his accusing finger at the stunned audience while his jagged white beard bobbed up and down, belching out warnings to the city of Nineveh that they are on a collision course with none other than God Himself. For olive skinned people this white skinned prophet must truly have been a sign and wonder.

Even before the interview was over, people were probably weeping, tearing their clothes and throwing ashes on themselves. The royal entourage example further enhanced the mandatory royal decree so the people would respond swiftly. Sack cloth and ashes was the ancient Middle-Eastern way of indicating earnest submission. It also represented a heart humble before God.

My two oldest children Grace and Pete are U.S.F. college students. When Grace and her roommate Sarah prepare for a home team football or basketball game they wear the strangest apparel. Some of their friends go so far as to paint themselves gold and green (school colors) and then top it off by wearing a peculiar set of bullhorns (the Brahman bull is the school mascot). It is their way of showing support for the local team. It was no different in Jonah's day. Clothes or in Nineveh's case, the lack there of, made a statement about where their heart was.

Right down to the animals, everyone repented. That may seem bizarre but if we return to the football analogy, even people at football games make their pets wear school colors. The Ninevites wanted God to know they were serious, right down to their last lamb. When Assyrian kings gave orders to their people, they were not to be trifled with, for ignoring a royal command meant swift punishment! Some historical accounts suggest that people were even skinned alive.

> *"No man, beast, herd or flock is allowed to eat or even to drink anything. But both man and beast must be covered with sackcloth; and let men call on God earnestly that each may turn from His wicked way and from the violence which is in his hand."*

> Jonah 3:7 & 8

As the inhabitants began to repent and cry out to the Lord for forgiveness, they were hoping that God would change His mind and withdraw His burning anger. They were not disappointed. Jonah had a different response which amounted to. "So they repented big deal!" They needed to be punished, after all he, Jonah prophet of God was punished! "Serves these Gentiles right, they deserve punishment," Jonah decided.

Jonah was not one bit impressed or moved by the obvious display of earnest repentance. The two groups were rivals, adversaries, opposing team and according to Jonah, did not have the right to ask for mercy. A popular T-shirt expressed the sentiment well, "No mercy."

God had a different take on what happened to the Ninevites. Jonah got two chances but continued to be stiff-necked while the Ninevites got one chance and repented quickly in the hopes God would change His mind.

Imagine this scene in heaven. An angelic watcher replete with flowing white robes, leans over heaven's banister. As he sees what is happening, the angel decides to get the attention of The Boss. Gabriel adjusts his halo, which was just put on tilt due to Jonah's bad attitude. He elbows his fellow angelic being and suggests,

"Look Michael, tell the Most Holy One to notice what is happening on earth to the Ninevites." He adds this footnote when he has the Heavenly Father's attention.

"Lord, look at what is going on in Ninevah." God sits back in His chair to take it all in. Then He commands that the angel takes his hand away from the "city delete button" on the heavenly computer. God takes another look. Good golly, Miss Molly, those angels are right.

"Wait," God declares. Meanwhile the Ninevites are weeping and repenting en masse. He reminds one of His workers, "If only My children in the northern kingdom of Israel had done this, and I sent them more than just one prophet."

God canceled the calamity for now and exits the 'delete' program.

Everyone in heaven sighs with relief and rejoices, curiously awed by this new and happy turn of events. For now, God has renamed the folder and added the Ninevites to His mercy file.

Hit the Road Jack

Meanwhile, someone on earth had quite a different attitude. Jonah hit the road and was traveling as fast as He could away from Nineveh. On his way out of the city he looked up and saw a sign, "Nineveh city limits 30 miles. Good," he muses to himself! "I have to get as far away as I can from this place and yet close enough to see the action. I want my buddies back home to know about the calamity that God and I caused on all those nasty gentiles."

"Me and Moses, that's who they're going to remember." The family will see that I finally did make good. I will be on the cover of *My Favorite Prophecy's* or the reality series, Destruction, This Was Your Life Jonah.

One last glance over his shoulder and he kept walking as far from the city as he could get with nose in the air. Methodically, he checked his "Prophet Catastrophe Checklist,

1) 2 minute preaching, warning Ninevites of destruction, *check*.
2) shake dust of the city off with his leather sandal, *check*.
3) lounge chair, gourd umbrella, binoculars, sunscreen and iced tea, *check*."

Wondering if he was far enough from the perimeter of the city wall, he decided to move his folding chair a little farther back. After all, it wouldn't do to get in the way of the volcanic ashes, locusts or whatever other destructive and creative calamity that God was going to heap on the Ninevites. "Whew," thought Jonah as he wiped his brow. He hadn't counted on it being so hot. With binoculars eyeing Nineveh, he sipped his ice tea and began to patiently wait and wait and wait!

Trial and Error

Even after I checked out of the hospital I needed to be dialyzed every other day. So arrangements were made at the local dialysis unit. The smiling staff checked me in as though we were at a summer camp. I had the usual mountainous stack of paperwork to fill out. One of the papers I signed, stated that I understood the consequences of a missed treatment i.e. death. This was certainly no walk in the park!

Reading the papers carefully, I became more acquainted with the dialysis procedure than when I was in the hospital. Every treatment I had to weigh in and then proceed to the waiting room until it was time to be dialyzed. There were always patients sitting after the exhausting treatment was over. When my turn came I was accompanied by the dialysis technician to a brown recliner. Sitting down, my treatment was almost ready to begin. Two large needles were inserted into my arm.

The needles were attached two plastic lines which were attached to the machine where the plastic tube or artificial kidney was. Extra fluid plus toxins were removed from my blood by the artificial kidney so that my body would not be slowly poisoned. Although the procedure was not an easy one, it always felt better getting off the extra fluid off my lungs so I could breathe better.

In the past I had always wanted to stay at my ideal weight but this was not what I had envisioned as ideal. It was a sorry and sad state of affairs. Each time it felt like I was going to prison. A smiling staff assured me this was better than the NO alternative. Now I knew how Daniel had felt in the lion's den, but having to go back to dialysis every other day was like having to go into the lion's den every other day. This was now my lot in life.

We are Family

I began the endless cycle of treatments. The following stories are examples of events that occurred during my treatments. An atmosphere of a clinic can vary from extremely depressing or positive depending on what was going on with patients and staff. The doctor in charge also sets the tone for the atmosphere of the clinic and more often than not they along with some other doctors or other investors, own the clinic. That is not to say that they should be blamed for every mishap, yet they are still responsible for the general handling of situations. As the saying goes the head directs the rest of the body.

During my two years I was in several clinics. There were numerous positive and negative events that occurred with some definitely better than others.

Rather than to single any one clinic and risk them being identified, I have decided to relay my experiences as if they occurred as though this were one particular clinic. It is not my desire to place blame but rather write about these incidents so they will give glimpses that will be specific enough to be informative.

As with any new beginner, the staff knows that some rookie dialysis patients can be a challenge. Early on, I was one of *'those patients.'* It wasn't the clinic's fault that I needed to be dialyzed in fact they were there to save my life. But I still directed a lot of frustration toward the nurses and technicians. I was angry because I had to endure this painful procedure every other day for the rest of my life and this treatment ate up what would have been family time. Plus, I couldn't compartmentalize this situation as it affected *everything* I did.

As the newest person I got the least desirable shift which meant my treatments began in the early evening and then ran into the night except for the days when I was teaching. The staff was willing to accommodate my schedule. But it meant that I came home late at night. Because of this every other day I did not see my youngest child at all except when I sent him off to school early in the morning. This went on for months when all I wanted to do was to take care of my husband and family and not to be gone. Furthermore, on many occasions when I was home, I was so weak that my children would have to come home from school and visit me while I rested in bed. Still they were thankful because mom was still able to see them at least every other day, even though she was sometimes very weak.

People have no idea of the difficulty, when one member of the household is sick. Despite the struggle, people often remarked how strong our family was. There were also many school and sporting events that I had to miss and the older children had to take on the responsibility of parents as we all worked together to stay sane and keep things as normal as possible on the home front. We didn't want anyone's pity we simply treasured every hour we got to be together. The wonderful result of this was that I got to know my children so well including their fears, hopes loves and dreams. So many individuals really do not know their own children and take them for granted thinking they will always be there. In reality none of us knows what tomorrow may bring. To really know your children is the greatest joy in the world.

Since everyone takes their treatments in chairs set up in a large treatment room, it was not uncommon to hear various conversations of other patients.

There are no secrets in dialysis clinics. Early on I had an object lesson regarding what it meant to skip treatments. Although people were aware of the dire consequences of skipping treatments, many took their chances and skipped anyway. It would be easy to be critical of such a foolish decision but sitting in that brown chair week after week there was also the revelation that good things vital to my health were being removed along with bad.

One young man, who sat next to me, skipped treatments regularly and was extremely unhealthy as a result. With his physical growth stunted and emotionally and physiologically unstable, he acted and looked more like fourteen rather than his real age of mid-twenties. His skin was an ashen color and he had numerous health problems. His attitude toward the staff was extremely disrespectful, which was not helped by his manipulative girlfriend. A former street dweller, she said she had taken pity on him when in truth she was busy taking him for everything he was worth. This girl had procured herself and displaced the boy's mom as his major confident. Through the desperateness of the young man's condition, this girl had weaseled and secured a comfortable lifestyle including a car, secure dwelling place and income.

She informed everyone that the two were planning a trip to China to buy him a black market kidney for $50,000. I thought they were exaggerating but found out sadly, that this was not uncommon for individuals with resources. Unable to be recipients due to poor health or poor risks, they are no longer allowed on the placement list to receive a kidney as they are already in short supply. Trying to speak conventional wisdom to these two was a lesson in futility. My heart went out to these two poor lost souls knowing they were playing Russian roulette with his life.

It was apparent to me from the general comments made by the staff, that they were more than a little concerned about his well being when he skipped several treatments. They often were in touch with his mom to keep her informed about his condition.

I think the candor of the girlfriend's conversation with me too made him apprehensive. On one occasion she informed me about the some unseemly details of their intimate relationship because she had health concerns. I told her this information would be best suited for the doctor on duty. These two troubled youths certainly needed a lot of prayer.

The "Young Lady" and "Big Mr. C"

To their credit the staff at the dialysis clinic tried their hardest to accommodate my schedule. I was put on the waiting list, just like everyone else and waited my turn for an earlier appointment. I was told there were no celebrities in the clinic. If you wanted something you just have to wait your turn. I was about to learn one of the difficult ways the patient got a more ideal time spot. Although I had moved to an early afternoon shift, I still desired the coveted morning shift. My turn was to come sooner than I thought but not without a price.

As I waited for my turn to come on the machine my path would often cross this older black gentleman who would be just coming off treatment. He was so kind and congenial and I could never remember his name so I nicknamed him big Mr. C. The capitol "C" was for Congenial. He always called me "the Young Lady. We had a lot in common because Mr. "C" was a former teacher having taught band for many years.

Sometimes we discussed sports teams "the Florida Gators from U.F. or his home team, Florida A. & M. Or we take a turn on where we would like to travel. Our favorite discourse would surround pieces of classical music and then our faith.

Maybe it was being called a "young lady," or his smart wit, but it was always a treat to be engaged in conversation with an individual who was intellectual and on the same wave length in so many things including faith. He taught me not to dread my visits to dialysis. Before I knew it, the nurse would come for me and I would wave good bye as Mr. C and I went our separate ways.

As a patient he always displayed the most excellent character, I wondered how he could be so pleasant and kind even under such difficult circumstances, for in addition to everything else he was confined to a wheelchair. He was always laughing, and telling someone his latest joke. He brought treats for the staff and always treated them as though they were his good buddies. Naturally, the staff loved him. He would have received an A in attitude if they could have given us grades.

I was just the opposite and I can tell you the staff definitely *didn't* love me. I was a proverbial pain in the butt. Instead of goodies, I toted around a little black note book and black pen to jot down anything the staff did incorrectly or poorly. I also noted what I perceived to be unsafe procedures.

I elected myself as patient advocate extraordinaire and wasn't about to let anything slip by. At a single bound I was ready to leap upon an unsuspecting worker to fill their life with grief and fill up a page in my little black book in case anything should go wrong. Staff mistakes were smugly noted and naturally I was duty bound to point them out as well as to tell them what they needed to do right. Always adding to my little book, they would hear from me, my doctor and maybe a lawyer or two. Unfortunately, there were more than enough incidents to record.

Like the bathrooms which were sometimes dirty or unsafe because of blood on the floor. Or not properly equipped with arm rails, toilet paper or towels. A time or two on a Saturday, I actually watched an elderly gentleman slip and fall because he was too weak and frail after treatment and not escorted properly to the waiting room as he should have been.

During treatments, nurses often called out food orders for the patients, like fried food, barbeque sandwiches, salty fries from Mickey D's. Since none of these things were on our diets, I duly noted that. A time or two the doctor ordered extra tests or charged me for a visit when all he did was casually say hello. As I pointed these things out to the staff, or challenged them, they were corrected. But why did they occur in the first place?

Mr. C. always took time to love and connect with the staff and didn't seem to see all their imperfections. When I asked him about this, he explained that they served us consistently day and night to the best of their ability. He appreciated the fact that they kept us alive by these treatments. I began to see things from his point of view but I could also see that he appeared to be getting weaker each day. Mr. C. saw my concern and decided to share his excitement over another special event that was about to occur.

He was counting down the days because in a few weeks, his wife also a teacher, was about to retire. He could hardly contain his excitement. Then they would have an opportunity to spend lots of time together and maybe even travel to some of those faraway places we had talked about. Whenever I would express concern or worry about him, he would always lean towards me and whisper these words before our parting,

"Now listen young lady, don't you fret about me, because my wife is retiring real soon and then she and I will have lots of time together." All of us, including the staff were excited and happy for him as he eagerly anticipated the day.

Mr. C informed me that there was only one week of school left. The next treatment day I noticed that something appeared to be wrong as Mr. C wasn't his old perky self, instead I noticed him slumped over in his wheel chair. I asked him if I could place my hand on his shoulder and pray.

I still remember our eyes meeting and those beautiful twinkling brown eyes filling up with tears as we talked. I knew he was in pain and wondered why something wasn't being done to help him. As we agreed in prayer, a very special bridge was formed between two Christian hearts. I felt convicted. Mr. C was kind, patient and gracious while I was an impatient, irritated and difficult. Maybe he should have prayed for me?

Unfortunately, the next treatment he was no better but seemed even worse. Curious about this I asked one of the aids what ailed him and she said the following.

"Mr. is truly one of our favorite patients and a wonderful person but we are all worried about him because we have to remove as much as thirty pounds of excess fluid from him in between treatments and because of this he does not fare well."

Another nurse who overheard us chimed in,

"His heart is so weak and he is not the least bit compliant with his diet. He eats and drinks whatever he wants. I know for a fact that he and his wife eat out every night."

I could tell she was frustrated with him. Then she added thoughtfully,

"But I suppose that given his health condition he and his wife probably don't have too many outlets and so their eating out every evening is something that is probably special for them. Still I wish that he'd realize that he is hurting his heart if he doesn't watch it. "

"Heart problem," I thought? *"I wondered why he had never told me about this."*

Now I began understand why He looked so sick and in pain, removing that much fluid each time from his body was taking its toll. That is why, when asked, Mr. C. would respond eagerly, consent, and thank me profusely when I prayed. One particular staff person who I disliked and had a major power struggle with was Mr. C's favorite technician. I was about to learn one of the greatest lessons from dialysis.

The following Monday I received an unexpected call from one of the staff informing me that a permanent place on the early shift had opened and was I interested in coming in?

"Of course," I chirped happily never noticing how strangely he responded to my eagerness. Why wasn't he happy for me? They knew how I longed for this.

I bounded in, ecstatic that I had finally made it to the coveted early shift but for some reason I didn't see my old buddy Mr. C. He usually was on that same early shift. I did notice that the atmosphere was quieter than usual. I was ushered in by *that* particular technician who didn't like me and who always took care of Mr. C.

Then he directed me with a particularly angry glare, to Mr. C's chair. I asked where Mr. C. was. "Why are you putting me here, I asked? Isn't this Mr. C's chair?"

The technician responded curtly, "Mr. C. died last night of a massive heart attack."

Then he added softly with tears welling up in his eyes. "And today was the day his wife was to retire. That is why you have his seat."

For a time during the treatment we were both very quiet. My eyes welled up with tears. I added meekly with a lump in my throat,

"I'm, sorry." He nodded in agreement.

Then we shared our favorite stories about "Mr. C." Reflecting on this event I think Mr. C would have been happy that his death had brought the two of us together. He wanted people to be able to connect and become friends rather than to stay adversaries.

But you can be sure that taking Mr. C.'s time slot was not an easy chair to fill!

I came home from dialysis that day after the news of Mr. C. and went into my bedroom and shut the door. It had been a horrible day. I fell on the bedroom floor weeping. I also had terrible cramps from the procedure. I wanted to die from discouragement. My son Peter was home on break from O.R.U. and began to bang on the door when he heard me weeping. I wouldn't let him in. I was ashamed and knew that God wanted to change me and make me a better Christian but I was weary of the constant obstacles and battles. Perhaps, it would have been easier if my life had ended and they hadn't saved me through all these procedures. Death would have been easier than walking through all of this day after day.

Peter continued to speak to me and insisted that I let him in.

He said, "Mom, I'm not leaving until you let me in."

Since he wouldn't go away, I finally opened the door.

One look on my tear stained face and he sat down on the floor with me. Looking into my face he said these words.

"Mom, when you can't believe for your healing any more, I can. I will never stop believing until you are healed." He finished speaking and put his hand on my shoulder and began to pray.

God had used the death of this precious saint to cut away at some of the callousness that had developed around my heart. If we allow Him to, God will use challenging circumstances to circumcise a fleshly heart, like the doctor uses a scalpel knife. It cuts deep and wounds but it also takes out the parts that are diseased, sick and sinful.

I knew I was in good company for Jesus Christ learned through the things that He suffered. Sometimes, it seems as though the circumstances take us on a road that leads through hell but just keep marching, don't set up camp there. I wanted to live and tell others about it. What words does one convey to say what an awesome God that I have come to know? As the song says, how great is our God.

> *"Although He was a Son, He learned obedience from the things that He suffered."*
>
> Hebrews 5:8

Another scripture instructs us, regarding our hearts.

"For He is not a Jew who is one outwardly; neither is circumcision that which is outward in the flesh; but he is a Jew who is one inwardly; and circumcision is that which is of the heart, by the Spirit not by the letter; and his praise is not from men, but from God."

Romans2:28 & 29

God had my attention. With the help of my son's prayers; strength and courage flowed back into me, making me realize that this trial was more than just one single person believing for healing. I had a whole family team lovingly in agreement for me to be healed. Then the Spirit of God spoke to my heart.

"You are like a spoiled selfish child. If you do not get your way then you want to take your bat and ball and go home. Get this into you head this is not about just you anymore."

I determined no matter how long it took I was going to keep fighting and with God's help overcome.

The bottom line to that scripture in Romans is that Christianity is not outward. It is not about what you wear, how you look or how many times *you* frequent your church building. Christianity is about **who you really are when no one is looking**. It is about your heart and where you really live. How you act and speak when no one from church is watching. It's the attitude of gratitude that is with you when you treat and act towards others with love, especially the "least of those," like children, older people, the unlovely and insignificants of our society or even the people that take care of you. Unfortunately, so many Christians do not know this but are some of the meanest spirited people. They have never allowed their faith to get on the inside of them and change their thinking. To them church is just another club.

Christianity is a heart thing not a head thing. Attending a church doesn't make you a Christian anymore than sitting in a garage makes you a car. Yes, I religiously went to church Sunday morning and Sunday night but observing a religious tradition doesn't insure that you have a vibrant relationship with Jesus Christ. Being a church member can be like joining the health club down the street. You pay your dues (tithes), attend the meetings and wear a certain type of clothing and even speak a certain lingo but that makes you a club member but not necessarily a saint. God is personal and when I say that, I have had people ogle and gawk at me. For some people even church people that is a fantastic idea. Christianity is more than accepting the tenets of a religion. It is acting faith out in everyday life. A relationship with Jesus Christ should impact how you live, love and express compassion to those around you. Mr.

C. had the trade mark of loving others and the possibilities of loving others were endless even in difficulties.

Having said that let me remind the reader that wonderful things occurred as soon as my attitude got an adjustment. For example my personal physician followed my health needs closely to make sure I was always taken care of. He even suggested that I change the clinic when he thought a better situation was available. As the relationship with the staff and me improved, nurses would share treats they brought from home or even a hand lotion because I mentioned it smelled nice. More importantly technicians and staff members would pray for me and encourage me when the treatments were difficult or long.

"God would see me through this difficult ordeal," they continually reminded me. These wonderful, loving and faithful people served me and so many other patients with all their heart. Slowly, my brittle exterior began to crack and I began to respond to love and caring and began to connect with the staff but it really was due to Mr. C. and of course my Savior Jesus.

Jesus was a Jew as were all of His disciples. The first Christians were a sect of Judaism. Two thousand years ago the disciples and followers of Jesus had all fled and abandoned Jesus because Judas one of His twelve disciples had betrayed Him. With a kiss and 30 pieces of silver Judas brought Jesus before the Jewish high priest Caiaphus for blasphemy. Jesus was then questioned and put on trial.

Since the Jewish authorities had no power to crucify Him they sent Jesus to the Roman governor to do their dirty work. Pontus Pilate complied unhappily knowing that somehow the punishment did not suit the crime. After this "phony" trial Jesus was laughed at, beaten and spit upon and then sentenced to be crucified on a Roman Cross between two thieves. He hung naked on a cruel cross. He died and then was buried and for what heinous crime? All because He said that He was God's Son. Every bit of Jesus life from the miracles to His immaculate conception, death, burial and resurrection were prophesied in the Old Testament. The Jews did not recognize their Messiah when He came. They rejected Him.

Out of fear and terror for their lives all the early disciples had fled each to their own respective home for both security and protection. They had no desire to follow in the Master's footsteps and get crucified with Him. Then what follows is the most amazing part of the story. Suddenly people begin to claim that Jesus was no longer dead but alive. Furthermore, they had seen the risen Lord after His death. Not just woman like Mary and His mother but other notable disciples like Peter, John, and James.

In fact, the experience of seeing Jesus was so compelling that all the disciples except Judas, who had hung himself, came out of hiding. They were convinced and begin to go into the streets of Jerusalem saying that they had seen the Lord Jesus. They begin to share their eye "witness" account with others and thus began Christianity.

Christianity has never been a religion but a relationship with the risen Jesus Christ. Since the age of 19 when I asked Jesus to come into my life I knew that it was a relationship but somewhere along the line it became a ritual of going to church every Sunday. In the greatest trial of my life, I had my relationship with God back. This was a faith so real with a God so close, you can experience His presence. This was worth everything I had to suffer.

He is wonderful, closer that your own breathe and He is more than just a feeling. God is real and you can know and experience Him through His son Jesus Christ. This is so much better than just a dead, intellectual religion. To be able to know that wherever I go, I am never alone; I can pray and talk to Him and He will listen, hear and respond. If you don't remember any thing in this book remember this. You can know Him personally by simply praying:

The Sinners Prayer:

> **Lord Jesus, please help me in these difficult circumstances I find myself in. I want to know you better. I believe that you exist. Please forgive me of all my sin and come into my heart and take me to live with you when I die. Thank you for hearing this simple prayer. Amen!**

Now He will take you through the worst circumstances of your life and will be your guide. You are no longer alone but you have someone who will always be with you.

This was how the early disciples survived being beaten and martyred. The early Christians went to their death singing praise in the Roman Coliseum as they were eaten and torn apart by wild animals or burned at the stake. Christianity flourished. Within two centuries, a barbaric Rome became the Holy Roman Empire. This was not mere religion but a relationship with the living Savior who personally guided them through every difficulty. This is at the heart of true Christianity.

The disciples insisted that they had seen, touched and communicated with the risen Lord Jesus. It was at this point, with individuals having a personal encounter with the risen Savior that the Jewish sect called "the Way" or Christianity began to flourish. To further distinguish themselves as Christians or followers of Christ they changed their meeting day from the Jewish Sabbath to Sunday the day of Jesus' resurrection.

His disciples said, "He is not dead but He is alive and we have seen Him." Other said that Jesus has manifested Himself over and over again and we are now His disciples. Their personal experience was such that they were unafraid of death. When difficult times came, they willingly laid down their lives rather than to renounce faith in Jesus Christ. Today in places like Africa, China and the former Soviet Union, Christians are still beaten and tortured as Romans 11:35 says "for a better resurrection."

> *To these He also presented Himself alive, after His suffering,*
> *by many convincing proofs, appearing to them over a period of*
> *forty days, and speaking of the things concerning the kingdom*
> *of God.*

Acts 1:3

From then on I didn't seem to have as many complaints about the staff and the little notebook was left home on a shelf to collect dust. I began to treasure a staff who tried to keep the moral high despite critical daily struggles. I realized too that a patient's request for the 'desirable shift' was a mixed blessing especially since the vacated spot was often connected to the death of a beloved patient.

Was that why the staff allowed patients to have chocolate and indulged them with treats from the 'no no' list? A disturbing revelation was beginning to dawn on me. They understood that for many of their patients this would be their last hurrah on earth before entering eternity. That accounted for the numerous allowances overlooked by the staff. I began to understand this as never before. The next week, my attitude toward dialysis was taking on a more humane approach.

The staff told Harriet that upon no condition should she ever try and offer a food gift to me especially a bright pink cupcake loaded with sugar sprinkles. Fortunately, she ignored their comments and decided to offer me one anyway. From her perspective the encounter involved a great risk as I had a reputation of being aloof and sometimes unpleasant.

I was picking up my book bag and about to leave dialysis, when a large black lady named Harriet walked up to me and offered me a cupcake. "I baked this myself, would you like one?" "Sure," I said. I took it and we began to talk. I was taking a baby step in a new direction and on my way to having my first friend in dialysis.

Chapter Review

1. **How do the Ninevites respond to Jonah's admonition from God?**

_____

_____

_____

2. **Do you need to respond and repent like the Ninevites? If so, go back and read the section that has The Sinners Prayer in it and then pray; remember to record the date for posterity here.**

_____

_____

_____

Chapter 10

Broken Vessels

○ ○

But it greatly displeased Jonah, and he became angry. And he prayed to the Lord and said," Please Lord, was not this what I said while I was still in my own country? Therefore in order to forestall this I fled to Tarshish, for I knew that Thou art a gracious and compassionate God, slow to anger and abundant in loving kindness, and One who relents concerning calamity.

Jonah 4:1 & 2

The Healing Anointing

Jonah had experienced the mercy of God firsthand but instead of being grateful he was angry, fit to be tied because the mercy of God had included Nineveh. It didn't occur to him that expressing this type of attitude might be a trifling inappropriate with God. Ever since Adam walked and talked with God in the cool of the evening and Abraham dickered with God about how many people it would take to save Sodom and Gomorrah, God's servants have always been able to talk things out with God. It is important to note that even though God sometimes has been willing to change His time table, His character and standards remain the same.

Knowing the many facets of God's character takes a lifetime. The healing power of God as well as numerous other blessings work in your behalf when His presence and anointing flow. Cindy Black's CD called the Healing Anointing is a wonderful selection of songs that bring about the presence of God when the listener actively participates in the worship. For God to work in your life means that you cultivate the soil of your heart. As they say, as the root goes, so grows the fruit. Even so health, is one of the by- products of faith.

Just because something is identified as an apple tree doesn't insure that it will be fruitful and produce healthy apples. The husbandman must prune, groom, cut and fertilize the soil around the tree so it produces healthy apples. For the Christian, this means submission to God, allowing Him to cultivate your life. As painful as this sounds, the benefit of yielding to the process, means being a fruit producer.

God is not a sadist; He doesn't want you to struggle endlessly. So get on with it and learn the lesson. There is no **one way** formula to get out of a health trial as numerous books suggest but as you relate to God, He will reveal the individual plan that He has for *your healing!* Each fruit tree is unique and therefore must be cultivated differently. Some may have a problem with insects or some may need fertilizer around the root or some may to have the branches trimmed. God has an individual plan to save each person by faith. But *they must* follow hard after God and use the same faith for healing to manifest.

Deliverance is simple but not easy. Do you want to receive your healing? Are you willing to do whatever it takes to be healed? I actually heard a woman say that she would rather die than listen to one of those faith healers and be healed. Imagine being that foolishly tied to one doctrine as though she had all the knowledge in the world. All of us must be willing to admit that we still have a lot to learn. We may even be wrong about some things we think that we know. Are you willing to make adjustment in your thought process if you need to?

Then read on and learn the many things that you can do to speed up the process and accomplish your goal. Think of knowledge as the arrows in a quiver that you will use to hit a target. How do you know which arrow will hit its mark? Get out as many as you can and direct them toward your target. For me, I kept hitting and hitting and shooting arrows, one right after the other. I was determined and persisted until I finally hit my target.

I acknowledged that even the determination to persist in seeking God or direction that produced answers came from the Holy Spirit. With all the strength and wisdom I could muster, I sought God's wisdom. Never wavering from the fact that God wanted me well, when I was given new information, I applied it with diligence. I am convinced that it was the Holy Spirit behind the scenes directing my life with that purposeful focus that finally produced the result of me being well and whole again.

When the realization came that I had no ability to perform the miracle, I was at the beginning of the end but didn't know it. Still I did everything in my power to cooperate with God's spirit and accomplish the character results needed. Each day I yielded myself to display the purpose of God in my life. In the end I could do nothing but had **created a climate for God Almighty to work on my behalf.**

When it was God's turn, it still took faith to believe that God would heal me. I continually waited on His timing, a slow process. Like the worm that spins a cocoon, faith engulfed me for two long years and in the fullness of time, it transformed me till I emerged as the proverbial butterfly. Heaven's cocoon produced heavenly results. When I finished spinning, sitting and quietly trusting, God healed me.

God came into the atmosphere, as I yielded and in that wonderful atmosphere I was healed. That is the part that good books and worship tapes play. They allow your mind to continually dwell on faith in God. Where faith is, fear cannot be. Which do you want the results of, fear or faith? I believe fear to be the greatest enemy of the soul. Both are creative environments, except that fear works in a negative atmosphere while faith grows in a positive one. Fear like faith pulls things from the invisible realm and brings them into the natural realm that can be seen. That is why God continually reminds us to, Fear not! Whenever I heard an evil report I put on my tapes to cancel it out. Eventually faith won out and its creative force produced healing.

> *"This is what the Lord Almighty says: 'Administer true justice; show mercy and compassion to one another. Do not oppress the widow or the fatherless, the alien or the poor. In your hearts do not think evil of each other."*
>
> Zechariah 7:
>
> *The kingdom of God is within you.*
>
> Luke 17:21.

In many Christian circles they talk about praying heaven down. Imagine how ridiculous. The kingdom of God is within. Let it grow in you to the point where it pushes out every evil thing from hell, every fear, every doubt and finally every disease. Let heaven displace hell!

When I was ready for my miracle everything in my life cried out for it. I knew it. I was ready. It was my time now but I could not manifest the miraculous that was God's part. I knew **my healing would come in the flesh because the Savior had paid the price on the cross.** But my part was to wait patiently on God and His timing. ***AND THEN GOD came and I was healed.***

"For you who revere my name, the son of righteousness shall come with healing in His wings,"

Malachi 4:2.

On August 28, 1998 at 5:30 in the afternoon I became whole. God gave me my miracle in the flesh but it was won many months before that in the spirit! Like the woman with the issue of blood ***I was made whole.***

Now on to the steps of Healing 101

Arrow #1- Confession

An important step of the healing process is confession. This Bible principle consists of studying the scriptures, understanding them as you repeat them over and over until they are memorized. You can only apply the scripture that you know. Remember to always check scriptures that are quoted from books and tapes to make sure the context is accurate. Once you are acquainted with the scripture, they can be applied *to your circumstances.*

First, I looked up and copied numerous healing scriptures from my Bible on index cards. Next, I repeated them again and again out loud daily. Soon I had many of them memorized. By saying them over and over again day after day, I firmly established that according to God's word, He wanted me well and alive.

As if to confirm this, precious friends Pastors Derek and Lorna Howard-Browne came over from church and presented me with a huge gift which they called a "Love Box". It was a large decorated box filled with little wrapped gifts. For seven days I was to open one of the gifts in the box. The gifts were all sorts of little things for the kitchen and home, like a lemon squeezer or ceramic spoon holder. Wrapped on the outside of each package was the real treasure. An index card taped to the outside with a healing scripture on it. I added these to my other scripture healing cards and began carrying this small stack of index cards around with me *at all times.*

If you were to ask my family or friends, they would verify this. I would be walking outside and a neighbor might ask me what I was reading and I would then show them one of my meditating scriptures for the day. Whenever I biked or walked, I would carry them in a belly-pack. When I swam they went into a plastic bag to keep them dry so I could refer to them after my swim. If I went to the store they were in my purse for quick reference. I determined that my mind would be fixed on God's word. Every free minute of every day, they were what I saw and thought about.   God and His Word on healing became my *constant* focus. That is basically how you begin to meditate and renew your mind to the word of God. Study continually as though you're next breath depends upon it because it does!

> *This book of the law shall not depart out of thy mouth; but thou shall meditate therein day and night, that thou may observe to do according to all that is written therein; for then thou shall make thy way prosperous, and thou shall have good success.*

> Joshua 1:8

> *For the word of God is living and active and sharper that any two- edged sword, and piercing as far as the division of soul and spirit, of both joints and marrow, and able to judge the thoughts and intents of the heart.*

> Hebrews 4:12

> *Beloved, I pray above all things that you may prosper and be in health even as your soul prospers.*

> III John 2

> *"For I will restore you to health and I will heal you of your wounds," declares the Lord.*

> Jeremiah 2:24b

> *By His stripes you were healed.*

> I Peter 2:24

> *"I, the Lord, am your healer."*

> Exodus 16:21

> *Heal me, O Lord, and I shall be healed.*

> Jeremiah 17:14a

> *And I will cleanse their blood which I have not cleansed.*

> Joel 3:21

> *"He Himself took our infirmities and, carried away our diseases."*

> Matthew 8:17

"Therefore, I say to you, all things for which you pray and ask, believe that you have received them, and they shall be granted you."

Mark 11:24

The thief comes only to kill, steal and destroy."

John 10:10

But Jesus turning and seeing her said, "Daughter, take courage, your faith has made you well." And at once the woman was made well.

Matthew 9:22

"You know how God anointed Jesus of Nazareth, who went about doing good, healing all those who were oppressed by the devil; for God was with Him."

Acts 10:38

Reading these scriptures plus others firmly established the fact that God wanted me well and that the devil was the one who had stolen my health. It is also my belief that these scripture established that there is a real and personal devil just as there is a real and personal God. Scripture contends that this personal devil kills, steals and destroys. Because I believe in the ultimate authority of the Word of God, I believe what God's word says is true.

What God's Word did was to lay a foundation and cornerstone of healing in my heart so large and so secure that no doctor's bad health report could deter me from what God said He had for me. Nothing I saw physically or experienced in my body naturally could move or shake me from this truth because now this was *revelation* truth.

True, my faith faltered at times and Satan attempted to bring me to my knees when the pain was great or the circumstances threatened to overwhelm me but by the grace of our Lord Jesus Christ and **revelation truth,** I kept getting back up. Something deep within that would rise up and buoy my faith up and encourage me to face one more day. The Holy Spirit will never let you buckle under and be defeated even against seemingly impossible odds.

God's Word had provided healing and that settled that. "Health is available for even me," I reasoned. "I will be healed and access total health by the grace of God." With that firmly established in my heart, I was on to the next arrow in my quiver.

Arrow #2- Forgiveness

By continually dwelling on the healing scriptures my soul was prospering and being strengthened by the God's Word but then I read a scripture on forgiveness. Somehow, I was not sure that I was fully compliant with this. My children had been in a Christian School and some things happened that were extremely vexing to my soul and unprofessional in my mind. God was not one to keep things in theory only. I had to forgive the school personal completely. It was not as easy as it looked.

There were many things that had been violated while at that school. For example, school records that my son and daughter needed for the university and the new school they were attending were held up for months. But God reminded me about how many good things that this pastor had done for my children. Count your blessings and never meditate on the negative side of things no matter how compelling. Make a decision to fix your mind on the positive. That became my focus. Never allow a negative mindset to undo all the good things and experiences you have had from any man because of his less than perfect humanity.

Imperfect flesh and blood is what we have to serve each other and God. God let me know that I was angry and my heart held unforgiveness which is sin. God reminded me of my own weaknesses, humanity and imperfections. Why do we demand perfection in others when we ourselves are flawed? I sat down and wrote the pastor a letter and sent a small check to his ministry. I had to be sure my heart was right. When I did that it was like a huge weight fell off my shoulders. Forgiveness is not a feeling but an action!

In order to have the confidence to believe for my complete restoration, I decided to do some more soul searching. Having grown up in a single parent home there was still some resentment and anger regarding this. One evening as my husband and I prayed, seeking and asking God to give us our health breakthrough, my husband turned to me and said, "I feel as though you still need to forgive your Dad." Before my dad's death, he and I had a wonderful and loving relationship but in my early childhood that had not always been the case. To make sure I decided to pray and began to search my heart to be sure I was right before God as far as my dad was concerned.

> *But Christ was faithful as a Son over His house whose house we are, if we hold fast our confidence and the boast of our hope firm until the end*

> Hebrews 3:6

"And whenever you stand praying, forgive, if you have anything against anyone; so that your Father also who is in heaven may forgive you your transgressions."

Mark 11:25

Unknowingly my husband had hit the nail on the head. The next evening when I did my daily walk I decided to sit down on a grassy hill overlooking the golf course where I often prayed. Suddenly, it was as though dark thunderclouds had rolled into my spirit and emotions. I found myself overcome with tears and anger. When my parents had divorced it forced my mother to have to work to support our family. She was no longer there when I left for school or when I came home for a lunch break at school. Without a mother to come to, the house seemed gray, cold and empty. I felt abandoned with no one to care for me and make sure lunches were fixed or dresses were clean and ironed for school.

The impact of this latest revelation was huge. Growing up, I remembered a friend whose mom was constantly doting over her, putting velvet bows in her hair, including a special school snack or even picking her up when it was a rainy day. The nurturing kindness of these small acts made the contrast and neglect I felt almost too much too bare. In a society where "Leave it to Beaver" epitomized the norm, with dad working so mom could stay home to care for the family made my home circumstances feel like I was a fish out of water.

Again feelings of reproach, loneliness and abandonment washed over my soul and hot tears streamed down my cheeks. I cried as I thought of myself as "Little Orphan-Annie" the child of my past. I looked up to heaven and blurted out angry words. "God, why have You cursed me? What have I done to deserve all of this?"

I sobbed for a while not knowing how long I was there. Facing the pond, I noticed the sun sinking slowly leaving a soft pink stain across the western horizon. A wonderful quietness and peace crept into my soul displacing all the anger and bitterness. Then these words came into my spirit.

"Child do not blame Me for your dad dropping the ball in your life. Each person has the decision and free will to do what they want and unfortunately his choice had consequences on you and your entire family."

God was right. So many difficult things had come upon our family as a result of my Dad's actions. All these years I had blamed **God** for a choice that **He** was not responsible for. My dad had made decisions that God's word clearly is against. So why had I blamed God? I thought about that and then another idea began to arise in mind, "God, how many times do people blame you for the terrible things that others simply choose to do?"

I didn't like it but in a nutshell I began to realize the responsibility for the welfare of my children was in *my* hands. I shuddered, thinking about the awesome consequences the children might suffer due to my decisions. I walked away that early evening with an uncomfortable revelation in my heart. Children suffer when parents make bad choices. I felt the weight of my parental role.

Meanwhile, night was creeping on. I hurried home. My husband and I choose to care for our children and come home each and every night. I also know there were parents that night who were making different choices and would *not* be coming home and oh how those children would suffer like I had.

The Great Equalizer

God had not forgotten any of this and was about to do something so amazing so wonderful that would more than make up for all the past suffering. God in any life is the great "Equalizer," transforming the past so bad consequences no longer hurt your future.

That same evening I received a call from my precious pastor friends Derek and Lorna Howard-Browne asking if they could come over. Derek said that they had "something" for me. I wondered what on earth it could be. Another package I thought as I greeted Pastors Derek and Lorna with my usual anticipation. They were always a blessing to be around. But the 'something' they had, was a message from God. I had not breathed a word to anyone regarding the 'grassy knoll' experience and the next moments were about to be astonishing.

Derek and his precious wife Lorna sat down. Then he began to share what God had placed on his heart. Pastor Derek took me by the hand and looked into my eyes as tears began to stream down his face. He slowly relayed in his South African accent how much God loved me. As he talked the presence of the Lord filled the family room, I too began to weep.

He went on to say that I was not cursed but blessed and then he laid hands on my head to pray. As he stood over me and blessed me I got this revelation that his blessing to me was as a brother in Christ, a priest of God and finally as a father. I finally had the blessing from a father figure that I had longed for my whole life. What was more amazing was that only God knew what had transpired on that grassy knoll. "No one else!" God not only hears our tears but the cry of our heart beyond even the words.

What God gave me was for my family too. Soon my husband, my children and I were weeping as the Holy presence of Almighty God filled the room. We basked in the tingling and electric presence of God. My soul filled with sweetness like liquid honey and oil at the same time. This liquid love seemed to overflow and spill into every hidden, nook and crevice of my once hurting soul. I was overflowing with divine love. Love had certainly lifted me.

Where there was once anger, hurt, loneliness and rejection there was love and an abundance of peace. Never again would I suffer from the feelings of abandonment that I had as a child. The old hymn came to my mind. The love of God how rich and pure how marvelous and strong; it shall forever more endure the saints and angels song.

A void was now filled with the presence and love of God Himself. I would never know the lack in my soul that I experienced as a child. From that evening to this day I have ever felt blessed and not cursed. God restored the lonely, empty and reproachful years that I had of being from a single home. That is why I say that God is "The Great Equalizer". Regardless of how overwhelmed you are from negative experiences in the playground of your youth, in a single moment God can water the dustbowl and fill up those pits and holes of your soul and make it a garden.

God's Secret Garden

In the twinkling of an eye God came down and with a strong right arm leveled the playing field. With his left hand, He planted lush, green grass, filled the borders with roses and lilies making the playground take shape. He reinforced the walls to keep out anyone trying to illegally scale the walls. Instead of tears and sorrow, joy and laughter filled the past. He made me to stand shoulder to shoulder as an equal to anyone even a princess. After all I was child to a king. From then on, whenever I recalled my past, they were of happy thoughts from the past.

I began to realize that the enemy had designed the current sickness to be a treacherous black abyss that would sink and destroy me. But by the same token God had reengineered these circumstances to take me on a wonderful journey that would restore the past. God's Secret Garden was a journey not to descend but ascend to the highest summit and pinnacle of the Christian experience.

Deciding to cooperate with God's plan holds a staggering opportunity. He will give you adventures to view His mountainous wonders and majesty while reveling in His mysteries. This is His desire for each of us. The enemy may whisper and tell you that God's good ship is doomed to sink like the Titanic. But in reality, despite the difficulties, you will be blessed beyond your wildest dreams.

Did you know that the Himalayan Mountains lie on the earth's weak fault line?

As the fault line shifts below, the earth's surface opens up to release the volcanic molten lava. When it does the molten lava cools and dries at the mountain base allowing these same mountain pinnacles to soar higher and higher into the clouds of heaven. So it is with our frail humanity. In God our fiery trials provide the building materials that form foundations that increase the heights so that we may can climb and soar with Him. All this is because of the great mercy of God and His goodness.

> *Beloved, do not be surprised at the fiery ordeal among you which comes upon you for your testing , as though some strange thing were happening to you; but to the degree that you share the sufferings of Christ, keep on rejoicing: so that also at the revelation of His glory, you may rejoice with exaltation.*
>
> I Peter 4:12&13

Arrow #3- Fortifying Your Faith through Family & Friends

The next arrow or stepping stone that God laid and placed securely on the foundation was to be constant in faith. God developed in me an ability to stand and stand and stand for the manifestation of the miracle as long as necessary. God had shown me that there was a time, *a perfect time* for my miracle to take place just like a wedding day.

Many things had to be done before my 'special day'. One of the ways this happened was through family and friendships that God placed around me. My husband Rick, the children and family were a constant source of encouragement along with some special friends. Each day my husband would place his hands on my back where my kidneys were and pray over them saying the following as Pastor Dale Brooks had instructed us.

> I bless you with life.
> I bless you with health.
> I bless you with quickening faith and strength.

My husband's faith and prayers did so much to encourage my faith. Also, friends would call to encourage me. Often times after church, individuals like the pastor's son Warren Brooks would come up to me and let me know that he and his wife Denise were praying for me.

Another friend from church Georgiana Cassala quoted a passage from the book of Daniel. "Three men were thrown into the fiery furnace for their faith." She said,

"You are like the three Hebrew children Shadrach, Meshach and Abednego. You have not bowed your knee to Satan's golden image and system of this world and when this ordeal is over you will not even have the smell of smoke on your clothes. God will deliver you from this fiery ordeal." Then she added, "This is a love walk."

She was correct. God was teaching me to love the unlovely. I had to learn to be around all kinds of folks of different educational backgrounds, social standings, religions, and races and to treat each and every one of them in a loving and forgiving way.

The king Nebuchadnezzar asked the three Hebrew children.

> *"Is it true, Shadrach, Meshach and Abed-nego, that you do not serve my gods or worship thee golden image that I have set up? But if you do not worship, you will immediately be cast into the midst of a furnace of blazing fire; and what God is there who can deliver you out of my hands?" Shadrach, Meshach and Abed-nego answered and said to the king.*

> *"If it be so, our God whom we continually serve is able to deliver us from the furnace of the blazing fire: and He will deliver us out of your hand, O king. But even if He does not, let it be known to you, O king, that we are not going to serve your gods or worship the golden image that you have set up."*

> *Then these men were tied up and thrown into the fire. The king's high officials gathered around and saw in regard to these men that the fire had no effect on the bodies of these men nor was the hair of their head singed, nor were their trousers damaged, nor had the smell of fire even come on them.*

> *He (Nebuchadnezzar) answered and said "Look I see four man loosed and walking about in the fire without harm, and the appearance of the fourth is like the son of the gods." Nebuchadnezzar responded and said," Blessed be the God of Shadrach, Meshach, and Abednego, who has sent His angel and delivered His servants who put their trust in Him,"*

Daniel 3:14-18, 21, 27, 25 &28

As I spent day after day on treatments, I began to memorize scripture after scripture. Listening to Christian music and scripture tapes helped me to approach unpleasant circumstances, difficult people and seemingly impossible circumstances with faith instead of bitterness.

As the days, months and ultimately years ticked by slowly, I began to change. God gave me the wisdom to know what to do and grace to forgive when I needed to forgive. As my attitude improved and newer patients came on dialysis, I was even accused of having a 'Polly Anna' attitude but still I refused to be negative. I remained happy and upbeat. I had faith and knew God was with me and that this horrible ordeal was temporary. I cannot imagine what would have happened to me if I did not faith and hope to believe that I would be well and made whole again. So many special friends took time to call, pray and encourage me and continually agreed and believed God for my healing.

> *And Jesus answered and said to them, "Truly I say to you, if you have faith, and do not doubt, you shall not only do what was done to the fig tree, but even if you say to this mountain, 'be taken up and cast into the sea,' it shall happen.*
>
> *"And everything you ask in prayer, believing, you shall receive."*

Matthew 21: 21

One day as I was taking Joy to school I noticed a small cornfield in back of someone's yard. Each day I would pass this cornfield amazed at how quickly the stalks grew taller and taller with the spring rains. I imagined my faith growing too as friend Mildred Branch had said. "Scriptures states that from a tiny mustard seed grows the great and mighty mustard tree." As the healthy corn stalks grew taller, I too grew believing, praying and confessing God's word!

Then, I noticed the tiniest corn ears appearing from that golden silk on the green stalks. The days grew longer as summer approached while the sweet yellow corn grew plumper. "Soon they will get to pick and enjoy the fruit of their labor." I thought.

But every wise farmer knows that right before harvest is the most dangerous time. The next day, I drove by the corn and I noticed something tragic. The raccoons had gotten to those tender plants. Oh, the sad sight of trampled cornfields, bent over stalks and all of that tender corn gone and eaten by varmints. This was another important lesson for me. Right before harvest time the farmer must be extra diligent, never assuming an automatic yield or he will never enjoy his produce.

For me that meant I needed to be extra vigilant with my faith. There was a season to plant, to grow and then to harvest. Each part must be watched over carefully with prayer! Satan is not going to sit idly by while you harvest your miracle. Right up till my miracle occurred, Satan continued to overshadow and cast doubtful thoughts regarding my faith. He suggested that God had forgotten me or perhaps I really didn't have the ability to have an answer to prayer. Maybe I was doing something wrong and wouldn't receive my miracle but soon I realized that many folks with a lot less faith than me had been healed a lot sooner.

That is when trust and your personal relationship with God are really tested. The Holy Spirit whispered to my weary heart. "Trust Me and walk on."

Each time doubt came to my mind, I would struggle to pull it down with every fiber of my being. God had gotten me this far and He would take me through this or I would die trusting Him to heal me. If I got to heaven early, I would point my finger at Him and say,

"I trusted YOU for my healing and here I am in heaven, what do you have to say to that, God?"

That could never happen because of what the Bible says. God honors His Word when we stand and stand and refuse to relinquish our faith. What really took all the time was the development of my character and beloved there are no shortcuts to that.

> *We are destroying speculations and every lofty thing (that is) raised up against the knowledge of God, and we are taking every thought captive to the obedience of Christ.*

2 Corinthians 10:5

To some if they don't get the manifestation of their healing they instantly assume that something is wrong and that they cannot be healed. That simply isn't true. Ask them if they always grant every request to their children immediately? Can you imagine how spoiled those children would be? God let me know in my spirit that He was not Burger King and I wasn't going to get my way instantly! What God did was to constantly encourage me. Numerous words from family and friends when times were discouraging kept me going until my miracle came. Even at night my dreams spoke of hope. This was a time of preparation much like Moses who spent 40 years in the desert.

My friend Cindy Perry said to savor and enjoy this time of rest with God. As time went on and I got weaker from the treatments, God provided a precious couple Dan and Amparo Burris from our church to would come and clean our house. They not only cleaned but ministered to me and prayed. One day Amparo said the exact same thing as Cindy had said. I was to savor every moment with God as one sucks juice from a fruit.

By bringing a small cassette recorder everywhere and listening to certain tapes until they wore out, I learned to savor the presence of God. Also there seemed to be places where Satan appeared to suck the faith right out of my toes so to speak. One challenge in particular was during the dialysis treatment. The presence of God will slay the enemy of fear. Confront fear with faith, hope with despair and joy with sadness. This is the secret of prevailing over adversity.

Arming myself beforehand with prayer, scripture and tapes, I learned that when those times came, I was to hide in the secret place of God's presence. Hiding in God is a formidable weapon which brings me to the next arrow.

> *For Thou has been a refuge for me, A tower of strength against the enemy.*
>
> *Let me dwell in Thy tent forever; Let me take refuge in the shelter of thy wings.*
>
> Psalms 61:3& 4

Arrow #4-The Secret Place-A Love Walk

Imagine having the key to an old wooden door of a secret garden. You put the key in the rusty old lock and the creaky wooden door begins to slowly swing open. You enter but notice the ivy has grown over the walls, wrapped itself around the vibrant roses trying to squeeze the life out of them when they should be bursting with color and fragrance. Each day, before the hot and steamy part of the day, you decide to take your key and escape to your special garden. Slowly you trim back the ivy, removing the clingy tendrils. You pull out the weeds giving the roses room to breathe and then shovel rich, black dirt around iris bulbs peeking their way through the ground. Working on your knees at first is exhausting because you are out of shape but time passes and you begin to grow stronger. You smile as water and sunshine brings the beauty of your secret garden to life!

Each day, as though the beauty of the garden was not enough, I had the benefit of a secret lover who met with me. His name was Jesus! Jesus, lover of my soul kept me through the horrendous ordeal. He kept me safe and strengthened me so I could face the world outside the garden.

No words adequately describe how wonderful the presence of God is but every now and again we catch a glimpse from the Word of God. No matter how wonderful your family is there are times when you suffer alone. Thankfully when that happens, you can steal away to the secret place. Through my tape recorder, scriptures and prayer, I built the wall of the secret garden brick by brick. I lovingly labored until my retreat was completed. Whenever life became too imposing and overwhelming I retreated there. This became my hiding place. Jesus taught me how to wield weapons of attack to confront the enemies of fear and doubt. I never knew where they would be found lingering and waiting to attack beyond the safety of the walls of my secret place.

Do you remember reading about the knights and how their enemies were dealt with beyond the castle walls? Evil knights would attack and prey upon unsuspecting individuals who left their fortress unarmed. Sickness and disease are two such enemies. But soon you will realize that by standing firm, wielding your weapons by faith in the cross and joy in your circumstances. Eventually the enemies of sickness, doubt and fear will be defeated and retreat back from where they came!

One day one of my precious friends Mildred Branch who called me weekly encouraged me with these words. Weeping she said,

"I see faith glowing in your face and like the rays of sunlight behind your back I see such tremendous faith growing."

She was right; seeds of faith *were* growing in the secret place in the ground of my heart, as I watched over them diligently, and pulling weeds of doubt and unbelief and watering them daily with my tears. Mildred and I saw in the Spirit, the small plants became a seedling and then a mighty tree.

One day even fruit appeared on the branches and they were ready for picking. To my amazement there was so much that I not only had enough for myself but for others and the more I gave away, the more they grew. Since, then not a day goes by that I do not have plenty for myself and others. Come with me and learn for yourself the wonder and joy in the garden of God's secret place.

As harvest approached, I knew Satan like those raccoons would try and steal my harvest. What should I do? I knew that I could not bring in this incredible harvest alone. God gave me my next strategy in the secret place.

God whispered, "You cannot do this alone. As you have labored together during this time, now call these same loved ones and let them enjoy with you the pleasure of the harvest."

I knew Dr. Serrano would say I shouldn't, but I decided to fast for wisdom and direction for my final breakthrough. Fasting is a powerful tool rarely used by the body of Christ. The answer came rapidly. I had no idea how close I was to the manifestation of my miracle. The Lord led me to call another friend who did something that humbled me. How does one ever begin to repay all the love and support given during a trial?

Arrow #5- Sacred Treasures - Communion

One day Georgiana and Mildred visited me and brought along some special gifts. As I opened them I found some sacred treasures. They were a crystal wine glass, Welch's grape juice, a beautiful small gold box framed with a picture of Jesus in the garden praying, and a box of matzos, to fill the box and the book titled, *From the Father's Heart* by Charles Slagle.

All these tools were necessary for me to get closer to my lover in the secret garden of my heart. Mildred, Georgiana and I took communion together and prayed. From then on I began to take communion regularly with my family or alone but I rarely missed a day.

> *That I may know Him and the power of His resurrection and the fellowship of His sufferings, being conformed to His death,*
>
> Philippians 3:10

I became curious to find out what the scriptures had to say about communion so I would understand more about what I was doing. I looked up the word communion in the book Cruden's Complete Concordance and made the most amazing discovery. Another word for communion was fellowship or agreement. In other words in God's mind I was performing the sacred sign of intimate spiritual fellowship and agreement with Christ.

"Another arrow or stone on my path to recovery," I thought!

At the last supper of the Passover feast, Jesus and His disciples did the most unusual thing. Jesus interrupts their eating by taking a common element and identifying it with unique significance so they would never forget. He took bread and broke it. Then he took some wine in a chalice and gave it to all the disciples even Judas saying these words.

> *And while they were eating, Jesus took some bread and after a blessing, He broke it and gave it to the disciples and said, "Take eat this is My body." And He took the cup and gave thanks, and gave it to them saying, "Drink from it, all of you; for this is My blood of the covenant, which is to be shed on behalf of many for the forgiveness of sins.'*
>
> Matthew 26: 28

In previous sermons Jesus had given them ample warning when He said they must eat His flesh and drink His blood. As good Jews, they were repulsed and horrified at the idea of cannibalism that Jesus appeared to suggest but still they didn't abandoned Him. They were probably relieved at the Passover Feast when He merely broke the bread and offered them wine. He hadn't actually meant that they were going to eat Him.

"Just more weird symbolism that Jesus is using to rattle our cages," Peter thought. Peter and the disciples were used to the fact that Jesus always seemed to be on His own wave length.

> *Jesus said therefore to them, "Truly, truly, I say to you unless you eat the flesh of the Son of Man and drink His blood, you have no life in yourselves. He who eats My flesh and drinks My blood has eternal life and I will raise Him up on the last day. For My flesh is true food and My blood is true drink. He who eats my flesh abides in Me and I in him.*
>
> *As the living Father sent Me, and I live because of the Father, so he who eats Me, he also will live because of Me. This is the bread which came down out of heaven; not as the Fathers ate, and died; he who eats this bread shall live forever." As a result of this many of His disciples, withdrew and were not walking with Him anymore.*

> John 6:53-58, 66

What Jesus really meant to say was that He was their Passover lamb, the final sacrifice. Willingly He went to the torturous cross for the sin of not just the disciples but for you and me and the world. Through His death, a new covenant was instituted.

In Exodus chapter 12 the Passover feast is recounted. At twilight on the fourteenth day of the month, the Passover Lamb was taken and killed. The children of Israel didn't fully understand what God was instituting, they just followed orders. Obediently they took the blood of the lamb and smeared it across doorpost, while the smoky aroma of the roasted animal filled the evening air. All of the lamb had to be eaten before they departed.

With the lamb in them and the blood over the doorpost, they fled Egypt and slavery forever. Disappearing over the horizon this wandering band of former slaves crossed the desert's sand and into the pages of Israel's history. I wonder if they were singing an old version of the spiritual, Free at least free, thank God Almighty, we are free at last. But God was not finished with the

Passover as the full meaning reemerges on the pages of the New Testament as Jesus and His disciples celebrated Passover.

> *So Moses took the blood and sprinkled it on the people and said, "Behold, the blood of the covenant, which the Lord has made with You in accordance with all these words."*

> Exodus 24:8

Now fast forward to the New Testament, imagine Jesus in the upper room on the anniversary of the Passover, speaking to the disciples.

"Hey guys, I AM the Passover Lamb," still they didn't grasp the message even after all the miracles they saw Him perform.

"*I am* the one slain from the foundations of the earth for all for you and mankind."

I am has come at last!

> *Taking the elements of their deliverance He broke the bread and took the cup of wine symbolizing His body and His shed blood and said, "This cup is the new covenant in My blood; do this, as often as you drink it, in remembrance of Me.*

> *For as often as you eat this bread and drink the cup, you proclaim the Lord's death until He comes. Therefore, whoever eats the bread or drinks the cup of the Lord in an unworthy manner shall be guilty of the blood of the Lord." This is the new covenant in my blood."*

> Matthew 26:26 –28

When Jesus presented *Himself* as the sacrifice at the Passover meal, the old covenant ushered in the new one. Communion was instituted. The disciples had the communion elements inside of them and the blood of God's perfect lamb inside of them. Did the disciples understood the significance and symbolism of this and piece this together with what He had previously said about drinking his blood and eating his flesh? Probably not but the cycle of Passover was now repeating itself in the New Testament but with a twist. Jesus suffered and died on the cross before their eyes on Good Friday and said this on the cross,

"*IT IS FINISHED!*" Jesus had once and for all delivered mankind.

Arrow #6- Faith or Foolishness and Presumption

I read and meditated on the Word of God, confessed my healing scriptures, took communion daily, forgave anyone that came to mind, attended every healing service possible including Benny Hinn. Each time I felt, this is it! I am healed but just to be sure, I got into the next healing line. Helpful friends had put me on every anointed preacher's prayer list that they knew including Kenneth Copeland, Kenneth Hagin and the prayer tower at Oral Roberts University in Tulsa, Oklahoma where my son Pete attended as a freshman. I carried around my own anointing oil in my purse. Numerous people laid hands on me again and again in church. With possibly hundreds of individuals standing with me and friends from church believing God for my healing, I didn't know what else to do. I still had to go for treatment three times a week for three and 1/2 hours a day.

Maybe I needed to take a step of faith. My doctor tested me every week for months because I expected this week to show a change, normally functioning kidneys but each time the doctor would shake his head as he sadly handed me the test results showing no change.

Against his advice I decided to take a step of faith and go twice a week for dialysis on Tuesday and Thursday. He discouraged this because cleaning the blood from toxins only twice a week was not healthy. According to the research for healthy long term results, individuals needed to be dialyzed three times a week. I was stubborn and adamantly reasoned.

"I must take a step of faith and go two times a week, then my hours would be reduced and I would get off completely."

But that didn't happen.

At first I was fine but as the time went on it grew more difficult. Between Thursday and the next treatment was the weekend and Monday. Sometimes there would be so much fluid in my lungs, I couldn't sleep. I even had difficulty catching my breath at times. I didn't get better but grew worse until I had to go back to three days and I felt so defeated. So what was the answer? My "Word of Faith" friends said that I must have faith and yet I felt as though I did. At one point I remember praying for someone with kidney problems and they were healed and yet here I sat on dialysis. I thought,

"God, what was I doing wrong?"

As I pondered these things in frustration, God was about to give me the answer. One day my friend Dr. Jim Etheridge showed up at my doorstep with a pastor friend of his called Lou who asked me a question.

"When you take a trip and you use up a tank of gas can you use that empty tank to get you home?"

I replied, "Of course not, what a stupid question."

He responded, "So it is with faith. You must get a refill of faith for each task."

Then, I remembered the words of Jesus,

"I don't do anything, unless I see my father in heaven doing it." If Jesus didn't presume on the grace of God, then neither should I as Pastor Lou had said,

"You must receive a fresh word for each situation. Ask the Father what you should do and He will show you what you must do to be healed." Pastor Lou suggested.

The lights went on. I no longer felt condemned. The Lord spoke to my spirit. "If you do the same thing the same way why do you expect different results?"

My daughter Joy says this is a sure sign of insanity, to do the same thing repeatedly expecting different results. If you want different results then you must change the way you do things. It made sense. God had given me my next key.

> *A certain man was there, who had been thirty-eight years in his sickness. When Jesus saw him lying there, and he knew that he had already been there a long time in that condition, He said to him, "Do you wish to get well?' The sick man answered Him, "Sir, I have no man to put me in the pool when the water is stirred up, but while I am coming, another steps down before me." Jesus said to him, "Arise take up your pallet, and walk." And immediately the man became well, and took up his pallet and began to walk.*

> John 5:2

How long had this man been in his condition? Thirty-eight long years! Do you think that Jesus saw him before? How many times had Jesus walked by him or had the disciples walked by him? Everyone probably knew this man just as we are familiar with the ones in our town or at certain corners that beg for food or maybe you drive by the same homeless person every day. This man was known because the scripture say, 'A certain man.'

He sat there day after day and year after year. If that is so then why did it take Jesus so long to heal him? Why did Jesus choose that day to heal him?

The answer to this question lies in Jesus' own words. Jesus never did anything without first consulting His Father.

> *"I can do nothing on my own initiative, as I hear, I judge: and my judgment is just because I do not seek my own will but the will of Him who sent me."*

John 5:30

As if to further confirm this some old and beloved friends of mine Ruby and Ford came over from Orlando. They told a sad story and cautioned me to continue to pray but also listen to the doctor's advice. They knew a pastor's wife who had cancer and she refused treatments because she believed God for her healing. She stood in faith and prayed and was in those same healing meetings but with one difference. She did not take any treatments.

Soon cancer spread throughout her body and by the time she decided to go back on treatments, it was too late. The cancer spread throughout her body and she died leaving two small girls and husband. I listened shocked and amazed but learned the lesson. Not only must I have to listen to God, to tell me exactly what I must do but then I must submit to follow the doctor's orders to the letter or be willing to pay the consequences.

Since then I have had the occasion to talk to many Christians about this particular truth. I have learned that there were many who died because they were unwilling to listen to their doctor. Many a Christian thinks they are in faith when they are really being arrogant and presumptuous. I pray God amends this foolishness so that they may live and not die to declare the works of God.

As proverbs says, Pride cometh before the fall.

Arrow #7-Fasting and Prayer

Kathy Muni, an old college roommate and lifelong friend called to check on my progress and to inform me that she was about to embark on a week of fasting and prayer. She wanted me to know that I was one of the major reasons that she was going to do this. All my pleading would not move her. My sister Darlene also fasted once a week for two years for me but to fast for a week was far beyond what I would ever imagine or even think to ask of a friend.

These sacrifices are very humbling for the recipient but they move the heart of God. Benny Hinny said the following.

"Whenever there's a need there's going to have to be a sacrifice to meet that need."

At the end of a week of fasting, she called to tell that the night she had broken her fast something amazing happened. They had been invited out to dinner by a couple from their church that they did not know previously. This man had kidney problems and was miraculously healed. This was the confirmation that she needed, to know that God truly had heard her prayers. The following night Kathy told me that, I decided to go out to the golf course and pray. I was weeping but the weeping was different. I wasn't angry any more. I was humbled, grateful and overflowing with the love of God as expressed toward me in the lives of His people.

I asked God something, "Lord I know that I am healed then why must I still have the dialysis treatments?"

He said something that overwhelmed me, "Yes, You are healed but you are not whole, you must pray and ask to be made whole." My mind exploded, God was right. I remembered the scripture about the lepers.

> *And as He entered a certain village, there he met Him ten leprous men, who stood at a distance; and they raised their voices, saying, "Jesus, Master, have mercy upon us!" And when He saw them, He said to them, "Go and show yourselves to the priest." And it came about that as they were going, they were cleansed. Now one of them, when he saw that he had been healed, turned back, glorifying God with a loud voice, and he fell on his face at his feet, giving thanks to Him. And He was a Samaritan. And Jesus answered and said, "Were there not ten cleansed? But the nine where are they? Were none found who turned back to give glory to God, except this foreigner?"*
>
> *And He said to Him, "Rise, and go your way; your faith has made you whole."*

Luke 17:12-19

Once again God had supernaturally intervened in my behalf. I had been given the final key to unlock the prison door.

I prayed, "Lord, please make me whole again," and then I added "if I need to do anything else please let me know."

The response came quickly, "If you want to be whole by a *miracle* it will require more time but if you want wholeness now then I have made a provision through the surgery."

"But Lord," I said, "In church I stood in front of the whole congregation and said that I would never have a transplant." I knew that was pride speaking. God was quiet. I now had a choice to make.

While thinking on all these things a friend and colleague Howard Johnston had told me a story. There was once a very devout man who read his Bible every day and prayed. One day a terrible flood came to his town. Naturally, he prayed to God for deliverance as his house was being surrounded by flood waters.

First, a lady came to him in a rowboat and said. "Jump in the rowboat and I will row you to safety," but our praying friend didn't go because he was waiting for God to save him. As the flood waters rose higher, he had to go to the roof of his house and again he prayed for deliverance. This time someone came by in a motorboat and offered to save him. Once again he didn't go because he was waiting for God to save him.

At the conclusion of our story we find the man clinging to the chimney on the tippity top of his roof. He prays one final time for God to save him. A helicopter shows up hovering over the roof with a ladder to reach him. He looks up at the person at the top of the ladder in the helicopter and thinks about taking the rope and climbing aboard to safety but then he decides against it. He declines while telling the person in the helicopter,

"No, I am waiting for God to save me!" Well, of course those were the last words of this poor fellow. He drowned in the flood. When he went to heaven and he came before God and said, "Lord, why didn't you save me?" The Lord said, "Well, I sent a rowboat, motorboat and helicopter but you wouldn't go."

The moral to the story is this. God sent the provision but the man didn't receive it because the package it came in was different from what he expected.

After thinking upon my praying hill for a long time I looked up into the blue sky and said aloud. "Lord, if this is really you then I want this to go quickly so I know it's you. I would like this to be done by Sept.1 1998 because it will be exactly two years."

For a week I cried and then was ready to move forward. In an amazing turn of events and in what was supposed to take months, only took weeks. My sister Leilani, who just happened to be a perfect match, donated her kidney to me and I was successfully transplanted on August 28, 1998.

Fasting can be a powerful spiritual weapon. I have several books about this subject but one of the best resources I have found was given to me by a precious friend of my family Victoria Unni. It was written by Patricia Bragg called, *The Miracle of Fasting*.

It has wonderful suggestions about how to prepare and do a fast from twenty-four hours to forty days. It also explains the different types of fast from just water to various tea and juice fasts and how it benefits the body greatly to do so.

Similarly, in Dr. Derek Prince's book called, *Shaping History Through Prayer and Fasting* some interesting suggestions on fasting are given. Dr Prince defines fasting as the practice of deliberately abstaining from food for spiritual purposes.

We must remember that God does not need to be talked into anything. What we need to do is to put ourselves in the position to be able to receive everything that heaven offers. Sometimes that means putting the flesh under by denying the body food. When we do this the time that we would use to eat we should use to study the scriptures and to pray. Our motive for fasting must be right also. Not for a religious exercise to impress anyone but in a true spirit of humility. After all God sees the heart.

> *"Is this not the fast that I have chosen, To loose the bonds of wickedness, To undo the bands of the yoke, And to let the oppressed go free. And break every yoke? Is it not to divide your bread with the hungry, And bring the homeless poor into the house; When you see the naked cover him; And not to hide yourself from your own flesh?" "Then your light will break out like the dawn. And your recovery will speedily spring forth; and your righteousness will go before you; Then the glory of the Lord will be your rear guard.*

Isaiah 58: 5

Chapter Review

1. **Which healing arrows do you need to apply to your life?**

   _____

   _____

   _____

2. **Write down a plan of how you will implement them into your daily life.**

   _____

   _____

   _____

Chapter 11

What Do I Still Lack?

○ ○

Therefore now, Lord, Please take my life from me, for death is better than life." And the Lord said," Do you have good reason to be angry?" Then Jonah went out of the city and sat east of it. There he made a shelter for himself and sat under it in the shade until he could see what would happen in the city. So the Lord God appointed a plant and it grew up over Jonah to be a shade over his head and to deliver him from his discomfort. And Jonah was extremely happy about the plant. But God appointed a worm when dawn came the next day, and it attacked the plant and it withered. And it came about when the sun came up that God appointed a scorching east wind, and the sun beat down on Jonah's head so that he became faint and begged with all his soul to die, saying, "Death is better than life."

Jonah 4:3-8

The Trouble With Nineveh

Jonah checked his Timex and tapped it a couple of times, to make sure it was still ticking. He folded his arms and patiently waited. Nothing happened. He began tapping his right foot. What was taking God so long? With all the trouble Nineveh caused others, they should have been zapped, toast, good-bye, finished all ready! As the sun rose determinedly in the east and shined brilliantly, Jonah began to mop his brow with a handkerchief. To make matters worse an easterly wind from the desert began to pick up. It was unbearably hot and sticky. Hot as Hades you might say!

He snickered to himself and thought, "A foreshadowing of things to come, God is going to send Nineveh straight to hell and I won't even shed a tear!"

Many religious people think just like Jonah. Have you ever heard some so-called devout Christian person eating lunch after church, discussing some project their pastor has suggested? "Heavens, why does our church have to be involved with *those* people? As if we don't we have enough problems here at home! There's no way I'm going to send one dime to help that group. If I'm going to help anyone it is going to be people in my own neighborhood!"

Sounds familiar? Even pious, but the trouble with this thinking is that these individuals probably aren't going to help even the ones in their own backyard! We have more compassion on endangered rhinos, whales, rabbits, chickens and pill bugs, in fact almost anything except people.

Do we really believe that people have no hope without God? If we really respected God's word, we would be doing more. Are you really sure that you have nothing in common with Jonah or the rich young ruler?

> *And a certain young ruler questioned Him (Jesus) saying, "Good Teacher, what shall I do to obtain eternal life?" And Jesus said to him, "Why do you call me good? No one is good except God alone. You know the commandments, Do not commit adultery; Do not murder, Do not steal, Do not bear false witness, Honor your mother and father" And he said," All these things I have kept from my youth." And when Jesus heard this, He said to him, "One thing you still lack, sell all that you possess, and distribute it to the poor, and you shall have treasure in heaven; and come follow Me." But when he heard these things he became very sad; for he was extremely rich. And Jesus looked at him and said, "How hard it is for those who are wealthy to enter the kingdom of God! For it is easier for a camel to go through the eyes of a needle than for a rich man to enter the kingdom of God."*
>
> Luke 18:18-23

As Jesus was walked those dusty streets with his disciples, a rich ruler rushed up to him and asked the Lord. "What do I still lack?" The response of the young man seemed to reveal a zealous heart. We can almost hear him.

"Jesus, I have obeyed the commandments impeccably but deep inside I am burning with emptiness, dissatisfaction and unfulfilled desire? What else can I do?"

But a closer look at his questioning reveals a justified heart based on his religious good works. He was rich, young and famous. In modern vernacular, he dressed in Calvin Klein jeans and wore Nike sneakers. He had a year round tan and dazzled the crowd when he smiled. He drove the right car to work and attended the right synagogue. This guy was amazing in every sense of the word but Jesus words went straight to the heart of the matter.

"Sell everything you have, give it to the poor and come and follow me."

"Was Jesus joking? He couldn't be serious. Give my nice things to dirty sinners?" Reasoning the young ruler thought, "How is this going to help me?" Jesus identified his problem. The young ruler didn't have riches ***the riches had the rich young ruler***. He lived for himself and Jesus suggested that he lived for others. "Come and be my disciple. Sell everything and give it to the poor."

Jesus' words must have reverberated in his mind. He gave the young man the answer that would have freed the young man. But for whatever the reason, the young man ignored the words of Jesus and walked away sad.

In our material world, this is an easy trap to fall into. Jesus by contrast was never afraid to connect and pour Himself out for all kinds of people. Saved, unsaved, Jews, gentiles, woman, lepers, prostitutes, tax collectors, Greeks and the list goes on. Jesus reminds us through this story that all of *our* great pious accomplishments are as filthy rags. They mean nothing if the attitude they are done with is self-serving. And it certainly doesn't bring happiness or fulfillment. It is in serving others one finds true happiness.

As the saying goes, it is not what you take from this life that makes you happy, but it is rather what you bring to it."

Sadly, we really think that this is how God feels. Before my trial I had a minimum amount of compassion. I had forgotten from where I came and what God had saved me for. I am glad God never tired of having compassion for me!

Jonah was no exception. So, God had to send another wake up call. It came in the form of a scorching east wind. Imagine after all this, Jonah was still clueless! Don't look down your proverbial spiritual nose. Most of us in the 21st century don't give a plug nickel for anyone either. Western culture is extremely self absorbed. That is why our popular magazines are called *Self.* Maybe the magazine should really be called *Selfish.* Some folks are so selfish and wrapped up in themselves that they don't even care for their own children.

God always has the perfect solution. There is nothing like a good trial to knock some sense into us. When trials come, the best thing to do is to redirect our attention towards God and away from ourselves. As we continue to seek Him for deliverance, strength and wisdom through the struggle, He is able to get our focus onto His will, off of ourselves and back toward others.

As we seek Him in prayer, He repositions our focus, so He can direct us to where He desires us to be. To find the place, where you were created to serve is the greatest blessing of all. Let me explain it like this.

I have vitamin E oil capsules. They can be used as a wonderful healing balm for all kinds of cuts but the oil is encased in a thick plastic capsule for protection. With a certain amount of pressure it is possible to break the encasing but if a person is not careful, the skin will burst, sending oil everywhere. It is much more effective if you simple prick the casing with a needle or cut it with a scissors. Then when the capsule is squeezed toward the opening, the precious oil hits just the right spot.

Either way the outside capsule is not going to remain in the same condition. You have to cut, squeeze or prick the outside encasement. Have you been cut, pricked or squeezed lately? Then, let the precious oil of God's spirit out. Others inside and out of God's covenant are needy for the oil that we possess. Let God pour out your precious oil as a balm for the hurt of others.

Enough meddling, let's return to our story. One Bible Almanac describes the east wind as an indicator of a change in seasons. Jeremiah 4:11 mentioned an east wind as "a hot wind from the bare heights in the desert." This uncomfortable wind was also known to be loaded with dust. Dust in your eyes, dust in your mouth. Dust everywhere.

The Bible's east wind might have also been what the Arabs call khamsin. The khamsin leaves people irritable unable to doing anything because of its oppressive heat. Imagine Jonah sitting alone on the outskirt of the city waiting for Nineveh to be destroyed while all he got was hot, sandy and irritated.

In the opposite direction, there is also a gentle western breeze that comes from the beautiful Mediterranean Sea. It is refreshing as the khamsin is hot. This western breeze also had the ability to drive off the biting desert wind.

> *When the sun did arise, God prepared a vehement 'east wind'; and the sun beat upon the head of Jonah, that he fainted, and wished in himself to die, and said, "It is better for me to die than to live."*

Jonah 4:8

Like the rich young ruler, Jonah learned that God isn't impressed with our good deeds. Life certainly does not consist of possessions that one has accumulated but in the intangibles of life. Each day must be like the day you got saved, looking for ways to do the Father's will. Jesus had compassion for the rich young ruler because the scripture says he looked on him with compassion.

The disease of self righteousness is probably responsible for destroying and killing more than any plague or germ known to mankind. One preacher said that attitude determines you altitude as far as spiritual things are concerned. Holier than thou do-gooders need not apply. True spirituality does not consist of being self absorbed but to be genuinely concerned with others and serving them. Remember what Jesus had said to the Pharisees.

> *"You have neglected the weightier matters of the law, justice, mercy and faith."*

Matthew 23:23

The God Kind of Mercy

Jonah was plagued by the same problem. No Mercy. Although this makes a cool T-shirt saying it is a poor way to live out your life as God's earthly representative. Perhaps this is what ails our modern churches.

Jonah knew God to be tolerant and full of compassion and love, yet he refused to share this understanding with the folks that really needed it. To carry the message to the people of Nineveh was what God had expressly selected him to do and yet he refused. Why because he'd rather preach about a God who destroyed the wicked rather than one who forgave. Too much work this forgiveness stuff! Let's just bulldoze the city and start again. Besides disaster looks more sensational and exciting on the front page of the news,

"Nineveh zapped by God with Lightening Bolt!"

It fits better with our sin and judgmental attitude but the fact of the matter is that God would rather rebuild, forgive and have compassion on people.

The earth is the Lord's and the fullness thereof. All creatures great and small the good Lord has made them all. All things belong to God and even the heathen are His and His inheritance if He so chooses.

Painted Red Lines

Upon the recommendation of Dr. Serrano, I was able to do home dialysis for a while. It still meant being hooked up to a dialysis machine for three hours, three times a week but at least I could keep an eye on the chaos at home!

At first glance, I appeared to be in control, like the Queen of England running everything from her royal throne or as it was in my case, the lazy boy chair. It would have been nice to be waited on hand and foot but alas that was not to be the case. In reality the kids knew I was 'tied' to the chair and that wrecked a unique kind of havoc and gave birth to numerous misadventures.

Anyway you look at it being hooked up to a machine with needles in the arms isn't a walk in the park but the children continued to have their friends over even though the family remained squeamish about seeing my blood pumped through the kidney tube. Grace's friend Leslie commented.

"In my mind I keep telling myself that it is not really blood but painted red lines."

In our defense we were just trying to survive and keep life as normal as possible for everyone. Like the time my ten year old son came in from playing with one of his neighborhood friends Tyler. With typical childlike thinking Andy and Tyler thought it would be cool to frighten the older sister Grace and friend Leslie.

I was about half way through my treatment. Naturally that meant I was hooked up to the machine with needles, resting peacefully. I was dozing while my dialysis technician at the time, a precious man, Steve was flipping through a magazine. Everything seemed to be going routinely until Leslie and Grace came screaming in holy terror through the room with the boys following close behind. The boys were carrying a huge black snake. Soon, I was screaming and jumping up onto the chair. The problem was that I forgot that I was stilled hooked up to the machine.

Chaos reigned. Steve screamed, "QUIET," while he tried to settle me and the girls down.

He promptly threw the boys out the house. The snake ended up being just being rubber one but it sure seemed real at the time. I shudder when I think of the mess that could have occurred with blood spurting all over the walls, carpet and furniture. Of course it was once again time for Steve to sit the boys down and give them a lecture on where bad little boys go. And so much for having a quiet and peaceful treatment time in my own home.

Then, one of my technicians named Paul was a jack of all trades. One day during the summer, oldest son Pete came home from work, there was no technician in sight. I jokingly told him that he would have to take the needles out of my arm because the technician was busy fixing the dishwasher. Peter, who was rather queasy at the sight of blood rushed into the kitchen to straighten this all our and found two bodies prostrate on the floor, looking under the washing machine that refused to work. One of the bodies was Paul and the other was my husband, Rick. Even though, Paul reassured Pete, that he would not have to take care of his mother, he did not see the humor in any of this.

And I am sure there was probably a lot of gossip going around the neighborhood, because as soon as Rick left in the morning for work, a young muscle bound man would show up three times a week like clockwork and stay for 3 1/2 hours. The next technician was like an angel to me, so I shall refer to him as Angel in my next story.

Angel or Cruella De-vil

It is frightening the opportunities and responsibilities that we have in the lives of our fellow man. The enormity of that part occurred to me when I was being dialyzed at home. My life was literally in the hands of another human being. A hundred things could go wrong and any number of these things could have killed me. One of the most wonderful and skilled technicians I had was an ex navy man who I shall refer to as Angel.

He made every treatment so routine it appeared easy. I never suffered under his care. He was gentle and sensitive to my every need. Before treatment became uncomfortable he would anticipate and make adjustments in the machine. He chatted with me when I desired to speak and was quiet when I grew tired and needed rest. He talked with me about scriptures or any number of subjects. One of his great loves was sailing. He taught me a great deal about fishing, boats and especially sailboats.

One day Angel did not come and I was greeted by another person much less capable than Angel. I shall call her Cruella De-vil because she certainly was. Almost immediately, I had a bad feeling about her. Although she assured me that she was a registered nurse, her competence and sanity were very questionable. She didn't appear to know how to hook up the machine. Finally, she declared she had forgotten something so she had to return to the office. At that point, I was no longer able to be dialyzed at home so I returned to the clinic the next day and who should greet me but Cruella. Grace usually did not come with me but on this particular day she decided to keep me company. What I had learned about forgiveness was about to be put to the test.

Cruella, a supposedly experienced nurse seemed a bit overwhelmed and confused about where all the lines went on the dialysis machine. After being hooked up to the machine for forty-five minutes, Grace noticed the blood in the artificial kidney was turning brown. Cruella began to panic and later we discovered that she apparently had put on an incorrect older artificial kidney on this newer equipment.

Somewhat flustered she took me off the dialysis machine,

"Is everything all right?" I queried.

"Of course," she shot back at me in an irritated voice.

By this time, I had not only lost all of the blood that was in the lines but also all the blood that was in the artificial kidney. Somewhat nervously I watched as she repeated the whole process again.

The second time the identical thing began to happen although for apparently a different reason. This time she had hooked up the lines on the machine improperly. Once again the blood began to clot off and I had to be taken off. By this time, I had lost an additional pint of blood. At the loss of two pints of blood, I was nearly going into shock. "Are you sure you know what you are doing?" Was what I wanted to say but instead decided to say something different with everything I could muster.

"I forgive you."

She began to flip out, "I do not need you or anyone else's forgiveness. I'm a good nurse"

The pitch in her voice was rising, "Why are you challenging my competence. I must be in control. I know what I'm doing. I will be in control"

Yikes, I thought as her emotions seemed to spiral out of control, I became truly frightened as she stood over me. There was nothing for me to do but be silent as a lamb plus I was beginning to get very light-headed.

By this time Grace ran out of the room for the person in charge. Another technician was rushing over to find out what was happening. Immediately Cruella was relieved of her responsibility and ordered off the floor. Meanwhile another technician was running down the hall, asking if further assistance was needed. All I wanted to do was to go home, I was badly shaken. Plus, I was going in and out of consciousness and thinking of the first dialysis with all those instruments against the wall. Was I going to be one of those casualties? Then I thought what if Cruella had dialyzed me at home? Again, God had spared my life.

Grace with tears in her eyes begged me to stay and begin dialysis for yet a third time. "Please mom, you know that if you are not dialyzed here I will have to take you to the hospital…you are very sick!"

Grace was right. I gave in and let them try a third time but was truly physically exhausted and in a weakened state emotionally.

I Get Knocked Down but I Get Up Again

Fortunately, for me they did not allow Cruella to touch me again *that day!* Another person had stepped in, to insure that the procedure was done correctly. More than five and one-half hours later, I leaned on Grace, arm in arm we slowly walked to the car. I was advised to write a letter about the incident so an investigation could begin, but in the meanwhile Cruella was still dialyzing patients and I would have another opportunity to meet her again.

Much later on, the dialysis administrator informed me that when they researched into her past records they uncovered disturbing information that Cruella had initially hidden when she applied for the position. After questioning her about the incident, they found out she was extremely unstable having been abused and locked up by her mother as a child. She had also been fired on an earlier job due to incompetence but this had not disclosed as the clinic was afraid she would sue them.

She was in major burn out which clouded her judgment plus she appeared to be on the verge of a nervous breakdown. Thankfully, I was one of the last patients she took care of. But at what price? I almost paid for this lesson on forgiveness with my life. And the importance that one person can play in our lives was truly brought home that day. I thanked God profusely for my wonderful daughter Grace who lived up to her name sake that day by saving my life.

Interestingly enough as Grace and I drove home that evening and recounted the happenings of the day a song came on the radio that was truly appropriate for the situation.

With the car windows open, Grace cranked the radio all the way up, as we screamed out the words to this song. "I get knocked down but I get up again. I get knocked down but I get up again; you ain't never going to keep me down."

It didn't matter how many people turned to look at us as we flew down the highway. We laughed and cried. After what we had been through that day it appeared to be an appropriate theme song!

The person on dialysis has a very trying life style. No one can say what worst case scenario is right around the corner. The dialysis patient is also reliant on the competence of human beings that care for us. The potential is there for the next someone to make a dreadful mistake that will greatly affect your quality of life!

At one point my husband and I were supposed to take a vacation trip. As the date approached, I had several nights of nightmares so he decided to cancel the trip. The cause was evident. How did I know if the person in the clinic had the competence to take care of me and what consequences would I suffer if they did not?

Heartbreak Hotel-
(A Pearl of Not so Great a Price)

The dialysis clinic was a unique place to learn about the tragedy of broken humanity. These centers seem to be scattered with the remnants of people whose lives have been crushed by heartache and misery. Georgiana had told me that I was like the three Hebrew children in Daniel 3, thrown into the fire but whose hair on the heads would not even be singed. She also felt that God had put me on a love walk learning to love the unlovely and would stay until I learned all the lessons that God wanted me to teach me.

One such person was Pearl, loud, vulgar and boisterous. She was in her late fifties and came from the local low income housing project. Her tall super sized body and revealing clothes boasted a once pretty face which now appeared hard and over-painted. After treatment, she would shamelessly position herself where everyone, especially the men, could get a good look at her. I watched her in disgust and thought, "Gross, I suppose at one time perhaps she might have been pretty but certainly not now." Attracting these men seemed a desperate act and futile considering the health of the audience.

Furthermore, she was argumentative as she was brazen with other patients trying their best to stay out of her way. At any moment, she could erupt, attacking any innocent individual with whom she had just conversed, for no apparent reason. Then there was always a long train of expletives at the end of any conversation.

She seemed to take delight in sharing loudly with no one in particular about her past weekend exploits with a blind one legged ex-sailor and other colorful types at the local bar she frequented.

In my mind she was truly repulsive. "How could anyone be interested in her and she probably had some contagious disease." Thoughts I guarded carefully to myself. Despite my headphones, listening intently to my Christian music and Bible tapes, it was hard to shut Pearl out. Unclean, unclean, was the song I hummed, for she was leper to me! Quietly, I whispered to the attending technician doing my treatment one day.

"Why doesn't someone try and shut her up?"

The aid responded, "Well we did try one time, but Pearl caused such a fuss that we almost had a riot on our hands. You see poor old harmless skinny, Joe who always sits besides her? Well she once bullied him so bad that he pulled all his needles out of his sites and went after her bleeding all over the place. What a mess we had until we were able to calm him down and reconnect him to his machine." I could imagine Pearl gloated over poor old Joe. Moreover, I felt justified in my condemnation of her until one day.

Fall shadows lengthened as the evening approached. My treatment was almost finished over, as I caught myself staring aimlessly at a lonely figure out the window of the clinic.

It was Pearl but she didn't seem to be her cocky old self. She was pulling the raincoat tightly around her as she stood alone waiting at the bus stop. Perhaps it was the fall time change or maybe the foreboding Halloween decorations dancing wickedly in the evening breeze, but I noticed a particularly sad face that crept across her countenance.

Pearl seemed lost and childlike, a poor lost lamb like myself trying to survive by the only wit and wisdom she knew. Suddenly, I recognized the Voice, whispering in my mind, reminding of the message that Georgiana had warned me about the Sunday before.

"This is a love walk that God has placed you on. Where you will stay until you learn the lessons that God wants to teach you. Loving the unlovely will be the greatest challenge!"

It was as though Someone had grabbed my heart. The squeaky clean country club lady from the right side of town was arrested in her tracks by compassion for the wayward lady from the wrong side of the tracks. As God pricked my heart, I began praying for Pearl. Bowing my head, I remember being ashamed of my smug attitude as one lone tear trickled down my cheek.

"Lord please forgive me for being so condescending and forgetting what it is like to be afraid and lonely. Please help Pearl to know that you love her too. Amen"

The fall leaves scampered in the breeze as the wheels of the bus came to a sharp stop. Pearl embarked and then slumped silently onto the bus bench, disappearing into the darkness.

The next treatment, to everyone's astonishment, Pearl was extremely quiet and even pleasant. I didn't think anything of it until something incredible happened. My treatment was nearly over when I looked up and to my amazement, who should be barreling towards me but Pearl. She seemed to be picking up speed like a locomotive train. Suddenly she stopped at my chair abruptly. With a determined look in her eyes, and a wide toothy smile, she addressed her comments directly towards me!

"You're a Christian ain't' you? I noticed that right away. You're always toting that big black Bible of yours around." I gulped and nodded, not being able to find my voice. The large intimidating Black woman continued. "Will you pray for me? Do you think the good Lord has a minute for Pearl?"

I nodded vigorously, "Of course, Pearl."

I couldn't imagine anyone in their right mind saying no to anything Pearl wanted. And certainly not to her face. After she left I thought of a dozen cool things that I could have said, if only my voice had only been there when I needed it.

Suddenly I understood all too well what Jonah had struggled with. Different culture, customs, values. Who really needed repentance? Many times as far as God is concerned both saint and sinners need to repent. Like Jonah, I really couldn't comprehend the full measure and scope of the mercy of God but I was beginning to get a sample as I extended it.

Fortunately, I had the presence of mind to touch Pearl's hand and had prayed silently for her on the spot. And that unmistakable blessed Holy Spirit that always shows up to validate frail humanity enveloped both Pearl and me. We were overcome and renewed by the conviction and love of God that day. God loves each and every one of us from the lowest sinner to the most self-righteous saintly hypocrite.

In the twinkling of an eye the Pearl of no great price became the Pearl of great price in the eyes of Jesus. After that prayer we parted. I never knew what happened to Pearl because I never saw her again. Perhaps God had taught me everything that Pearl needed to teach me.

The dialysis clinic always gave plenty of opportunities to remember that I was a Christian under construction. But it was time to travel on to my final destination although I didn't know it at the time. Under the supervision of my dear friend Dr. Gus Serrano I moved again because Dr. Serrano had opened a dialysis clinic. Of all clinics, I am glad to have finished at his because it was where the best treatments were given. Dr. Serrano's clinic was by far, the cleanest, the best supervised and in my opinion the safest.

The Race is On

I was finally able to secure the coveted early morning shift and God was about to see to it that there were 'adventures a plenty.' The earlier I got there, the sooner I got on for treatment. The sooner I got *on* treatment the sooner I *got off treatment.* I decided to be the first one on and off so I got there five minutes early. Naturally, Ivory, being a good natured technician, always hooked up whoever showed up first for treatment.

Soon, I found that a gentleman whose wife Barbara was being treated next to me. But he was beating my time by five minutes, so Barbara was the first one to be put on. Secretly, I knew Ivory preferred hooking me up first, because of all of Barbara's health problems and difficulties.

But Barbara's husband was a whiner. So, he would complain to Mickey, the nurse in charge, so poor Ivory had to put his wife on first. But I was not to be trifled with and *I* was determined to be first! I really didn't mind that much because Barbara was treated for four+ hours and always went much longer than I did even if I was not put on first. But it was just the idea that he would do that. It made me mad.

Barbara was one of the sweetest individuals that you could ever want to meet. By the end of treatment, however, she was always crying with the pain, or even screaming for help during her last hour of dialysis. As time went on, it was clear that her treatments were not going well. And we would always pray together because of all pain she was in.

But I was the competitive type. I determined to try and still be the first one to be put on treatment. The race was on.

So, I decided to get there twenty minutes early. Whenever we saw each other we would race to the door of the clinic to see who would be first in line. Then, the following Wednesday, I turned my car into the clinic and who should I see but Barbara's car. Her husband had gotten her there thirty minutes early.

Poor Barbara was a very sweet and a gentle soul. As soon as her husband left, she would always apologize as she was embarrassed by her husband but he was an ex army sergeant and not used to being beat. "If I had my way, I would let you win every time, Eileen," she said.

She tried to make me feel better. "Oh, that's o.k. Barbara." I would say.

But it was just the idea that he was cheating, that got to me. Soon we were getting to the clinic about forty-five minutes early. I do admit that perhaps things were getting a bit out of hand. Something had to be done because poor Ivory said that she refused to start work an hour early. She asked if Mickey would speak to me one morning after my shift.

Mickey explained that since Barbara had become sick their lives were completely out of control. Barbara's husband had always been in control of everything. He had a firm hand on the affairs of their life until the sickness came to claim his wife. She suggested that perhaps just this once and since I was relatively healthy I could give him something that he could win at.

From then on guess who always won the race? Barbara. A few weeks after that I notice that Barbara's chair was empty. Soon after that, her big tough husband came in to visit Mickey crying like a baby. Barbara had passed away peacefully in her sleep the evening before. In more ways than one, I guess she really had won the race after all.

The Final Quest

My good friend Freda said something to me that I will never forget.

"There is an end to all things." My time on dialysis was about to be finished. As Georgiana had predicted, I had learned to love the unlovely. In Exodus 12 we read about the children of Israel. God had given them their marching orders. They were about to leave Egypt and their slavery forever.

So it was with me. I knew in my spirit although I couldn't say why or how, my time was at hand. God in His mercy gave me one final task, a mission of love and great joy.

Miss Delores now occupied the chair that Barbara once had. She was unlike anyone I had ever met. Although she was probably in her early sixties she was still beautiful, and one of the most loving Christian ladies I had ever met. We shared many wonderful visits together. Each treatment day, I eagerly waited for her husband to bring her in, so we could catch up on all the current happenings of her life. Then we would chatter like two magpies.

Miss Dolores loved beautiful clothes and took enormous pride in how she dressed. Every day she looked like she was ready to attend a garden party with all her accessories matching. Sometimes she chose an exotic outfit from her regal African roots. Naturally her jewelry, shoes and purse always matched. Her beautiful ebony skin showed off perfect white pearly teeth whenever her musical laugh came forth. There was always an abundance of new stories about a newest baby in the family or a neat wedding outfit she was planning to wear.

She especially loved to wear these beautiful big hats and eagerly shared some new style of hat from a magazine of fashion long past. Occasionally she would give with me the secrets of a soul food recipe that she knew. Best times of all were the times when Miss Delores had a new revelation about something she learned from God's Word. One day she lamented that hats were getting too expensive for retirees on a budget.

How I loved to talk with Miss Dolores, for she made the hours at clinic fly by and so much easier to bear. One day Clark, our muscular, body builder, supply technician had given me a collard green recipe and I wanted to check with Miss Delores about the particulars but she didn't seem too enthused about it.

Again, later in the week, I tried to engage her in conversation about an idea I had for bringing goodies for the staff who worked so hard to serve and love us but all she did was turn her head aside. Ivory recently had given me a new bottle of her favorite hand lotion. I tried to entice Miss Dolores by putting some on her hands she sniffed indifferently and stared off in space. One who had given and sowed so much joy, graciousness and kindness into others was about to reap a harvest of love.

As I thought about how Ms. Dolores was behaving, God's Spirit brought to mind how much I had changed. Was I the same woman who had been so aloof, and distant? Now I didn't mind being surrounded by my new family whether they dwelt in the inner city or affluent suburbs. The cultures of Tampa were no longer strange but comfortable and fascinating. I had adjusted to my new environment but for some reason couldn't get Miss Delores off my mind. I wanted to do something to get Miss Delores back to her old happy self. I talked with Theresa the secretary who mentioned the clinic administrator too had been concerned. Depression for the dialysis patient was always lurking around the corner. Like the rattlesnake waiting on a trail in the woods for an unsuspecting traveler, one never knew who would be bitten next. Miss Dolores seemed to be the newest victim.

Miss Delores continued to withdraw from conversations and company. As I was prayed for her one day, an idea sprang into my head to bring her something. Still I wondered, "What would be appropriate for her?" The thought of a hat sprang into my mind almost immediately but what kind of hat? My youngest daughter Joy and I went to J.C. Penny's to look at hats and try them on. It was ridiculous. The more we tried, the sillier we looked. We knew nothing about hats because we were not hat people. Plus they all seemed gaudy and as Ms. Delores had said, overpriced. Still the thought persisted.

One day after clinic, with Miss Delores hardly looking at me, I determined to complete my mission. As I headed home that day, I was so fixed upon prayer about Ms. Delores that I missed my exit on I-75. Heading to the next exit, I remembered a friend's shop called, "Exchanging Hands." Since I hadn't seen the owner Lorraine in a while, I decided to stop in. As soon as I opened the shop door something stopped me in my tracks.

I knew that God had allowed me to miss my exit. It had not been a mistake but a miracle for I found myself looking straight back to a shelf that held the neatest and most unusual hat I had ever seen. It was gorgeous. Black and red with a smart looking gold band with bow around it. I went straight to it. Joanne, Loraine's assistant asked me if I wanted to try it on.

When I told her why I was interested we both had tears in our eyes and goose bumps running up and down our arms. We knew this was for Miss Delores. Joanne wrapped it in the most beautiful hat box I had ever seen and then placed a great big pink bow around it.

I couldn't wait till Friday. This time when I went to clinic, I was so excited. With the box on my lap I waited for my friend. But Ms. Delores seemed unusually late this morning. Then another thought came, "Oh no, what if she does not come, what if something has happened to her and then again what if she does? How am I ever going to justify such a gift?"

Laughing to myself, I came up with a silly idea or so I thought,

"I know, I will play a trick on her and sing happy birthday to you and we will both laugh." Time went by but still no Delores. I began to panic. Then all of sudden there came Ms. Delores rushing to her chair embarrassed. In all the time I knew her it was the only time that Miss Delores had ever over slept. I sang my silly birthday song and when I did something amazing happened. Miss Delores stared at me, her eyes got very wide and she said, "How did you know it was my birthday?"

I said "What? You mean it really is your birthday?"

Then I got even more excited, "Miss. Delores, I did not know it was your birthday but the Lord did and he really loves you very much. If he cares enough to know exactly when your birthday is then I guess he can take care of any other problem that you may be worrying about."

She tore open the box and squealed with laughter when she saw it. Immediately, she took it out and tried it on. Not only did it fit her but it perfectly matched her outfit. Tears and the biggest smile spread across her face, my old friend Delores was back and better than ever.

As if that was not enough, Miss Delores told me that she decided to wear her beautiful new hat with a white suit to church the following Sunday. When she did something amazing happened. The pastor said she looked so sharp, he asked her to come up to the front and pray for everyone. When she did the Spirit of God hit her and then the church. Many were saved and rededicated their lives to the Lord. From that day on Miss Delores was a new person.

All from just a new hat!

After that incident something really broke within me. I felt the Lord saying that my time at the clinic was over. Within weeks of that experience, I was being cleared for a transplant. As if to reinforce that, one day out of the blue, I received a beautiful bouquet of pink roses from my precious friends Pastors Derek and Lorna Howard-Browne. The beautiful hat that I had sown for Miss Delores' breakthrough had turned into a dozen roses for my own. And although I wasn't a hat person, I definitely was a rose person!

Chapter Review

1. **Why was Jonah so upset about?**

    _____

    _____

    _____

2. **What example in the chapter lets us know that God is interested in the details of our life?**

    _____

    _____

    _____

3. **What are some of the concerns that you need to take to God in prayer today? Pause and commit them to prayer right now.**

    _____

    _____

    _____

Chapter 12

Worming Your Way Forward

○ ○

Then God said to Jonah, "Do you have good reason to be angry about the plant?" And he said, "I have good reason to be angry, even to death." Then the Lord said, "You had compassion on the plant for which you did not work, and for which you did not cause to grow, which came up overnight and perished overnight. And should I not have compassion on Nineveh, the great city in which there are more than 120,000 persons who did not know their right and left hand, as well as many animals?"

Jonah 4:9-11

The Trouble With Jonah

God was not about to let an itinerant preacher sit on the proverbial back side of the desert watching a part of His creation go to hell. God does not believe in wasting any lives, neither Jews not Gentiles. We do not make the decision on who has quality of life is more valuable to God either.

Jonah needed to learn some additional things about the character of God. "Don't put me in a box," God seemed to whisper in the East Wind! But that was too subtle for Jonah. There are times when God does appear to be in a box. Like the time when the Lord instructed Moses to construct a sanctuary so He would dwell between the cherubim on the mercy seat while Israel journeyed to the promise land.

"And there I will meet with you, and from above the mercy seat, from between the two cherubim which are upon the ark of the

testimony, I will speak to you about all that I will give you in commandment for the sons of Israel."

Exodus 25:22

But living in a box was not God's ultimate plan. He wanted to commune with man and have a relationship so that man could know God intimately. God desire has always been to reside in the human heart, to be the center of man's existence. God's plan has always been to direct man from within, not just externally conform to some Old Testament Law.

Being manifested that you are a letter of Christ, cared for by us, written not with ink, but with the Spirit of the living God, not on tablets of stone, but on tablet s of the human heart."

II Corinthians 3:3

With God's new residence in mind came enormous changes in the responsibility and the ultimate value associated with mankind. In the past, God's ways seemed simple and predictable. If you did something bad, you were destroyed, if you did something good you were blessed. But man knew intuitively that there was more to his Creator than that.

God's actual nature even involved the smallest creature on earth, the sparrow. God's plan for humanity was to experience and be introduced to a philosophy whose central theme was grace and mercy. Jonah was positioned by God in the perfect threshold of time, to open the door to a whole new relationship because the time was at hand.

"Behold days are coming," declares the Lord, "I will make a new covenant with the House of Israel and with the house of Judah, not like the covenant which I made with their fathers in the day I took them by the hand to bring them out of the land of Egypt, My covenant which they broke, although I was a husband to them," declares the Lord. "But this covenant which I will make with the house of Israel after those days," declares the Lord, I will be their God, and they shall be My people. "And they shall not teach again, each man his neighbor and each man his brother, saying, 'Know the Lord,' for they shall all know Me, from the least of them to the greatest of them," declares the Lord, "for I will forgive their iniquity, and their sin I will remember no more."

Jeremiah 31:31-34

Our last chapter of Jonah opens with an interesting footnote.

"For I knew that Thou art a gracious and compassionate God, slow to anger and abundant in loving kindness, and One who relents concerning calamity."

Jonah 4:1

Most of us would have to spend much more time on our knees in order to understand the breadth of God's mercy. The extent to which God will forgive someone is staggering. Sure, we know God forgave *us* but that He should forgive others still surprises and confuses the church. Forgiveness from God is theoretically fine but more challenging especially if it directly involves us. We mentally accent to restoration in theory but in reality when God tells us to go and forgive someone who has done wrong and then reinstate them, we struggle like crazy. Yet, God never expects us to do what He will not! If He can forgive us seven times seventy, then that is what He expects from us.

God wanted Jonah to understand the extent of His forgiveness. This in short is the moral to our story. We know the prophet had an attitude and chip on his shoulder and reluctantly conceded that he understood the ramifications of his preaching all along. He knew God's, mercy to all sinners was the bottom line. If we paraphrased Jonah, we might get something like this,

"God do what you need to do, just don't drag me into it."

After all Jonah was a patriotic and prejudiced Jew who didn't want to preach to Gentiles, but ended up delivering God's message of judgment to a nation who represented the *Who's Who* of idolatry. That is why he waited outside the city to see if God would destroy the Ninevites as he had said. After all that would have been a fitting final triumph for a prophet with a less than stellar record. Unfortunately, that did not happen. Something unimaginable even worst than death occurred when the heathens repented and God had a change of heart, sparing them. What worst fate could have befallen Jonah?

Poor old Jonah can't get any respect! Trying to keep his prophetic friends from despising him for going to the enemy was going to be difficult. If they only knew what torment and humiliation he had suffered. You can be sure, he went home complaining all the way and rubbing his sunburned forehead, pointing out bunions and kibitzing to his friends about all he suffered at the hands of God.

The mercy that God *revealed to* and *through* Jonah was staggering. To a limited extent Jonah understood mercy because he had delivered enough prophecies threatening judgment against the rebellious nation of Israel and yet the nation remained intact. Jonah knew Israel's idolatry should have incurred God's wrath. Perhaps their disobedience affected him, causing him to believe that he too could dodge a difficult assignment without incurring consequences.

But Jonah witnessed an aspect of God's mercy that even He could never have imagined. The book of Jonah is short and appears to break with norms, moving outside of the experience of this well seasoned prophet. God crosses cultures, prejudices and religious idolatry to go to a despised and hated enemy of Israel to reveal just how awesome and extensive his mercy is. And when they repented, disaster was averted.

> *Who can possibly comprehend the mercy of God? Truly, it is new every morning; Great is your faithfulness.*

> Lamentations 3:23

Although, Jonah resented his new assignment, he was smart enough to record it. The message embodies something about the essence of who God is: His mercy, His love and His compassion. Jonah experienced the mercy of God in four short chapters. By contrast God instructs the prophet in five short, sweet and to the point sentences. The lesson **is the assignment.** When Jonah responds, it is in long, tedious religious discourses defending and justifying himself. Something like "I, Jonah a prophet, lest I incur further wrath from God and take another trip to hell, shaped up and obeyed God albeit reluctantly and preached to the Ninevites. Judge me not lest ye be judged." He didn't say that but he could have.

He ends his book in the best way possible, with God's word alone. If anyone wants to question the assignment, they can take it up with God! To Jonah's credit, his healthy fear of God had returned. His assignment was completed and recorded for posterity. In the end, his final reward was to be sent back to friends with a whale of a story!

> *"Shouldn't I have mercy on Nineveh, the great city in which there are more than 120,000 persons who don't know the difference between their right and left hand, as well as many animals?"*

> Jonah 4:11

Chapter Review

1. **Give a brief summary of what the moral to the story of Jonah is?**

   _____

   _____

   _____

Chapter 13

There's a Lesson to be Learned

Power of Prayer

In July of 1997 I had an unusual dream. I was a new recruit in a military training camp. The new recruits moved from station to station as they were tested. Each station had various hurdles that had to be successfully completed. One station however appeared to be more formidable than all the others.

The person in charge was a strong woman dressed in fatigues. Intimidation and fear was the major weapon that she succeeded in using against recruits. She took down every recruit that she sparred with. No one I saw ever defeated her. As I watched her, I thought, "You are not as big and tough as you think."

Suddenly, with unexpected heavenly zeal, I broke from the ranks and ran at her with every ounce of strength I possessed. Upon reaching her, instead of sparring, I placed my hands upon her forehead and prayed. This tactic so confused her that she dropped to her knees. Then, I wrestled her all the way down and before she knew what had happened I put her arms behind her back. She broke then and there.

While she was recovering from the shock of being beaten, I took this opportunity took look at her and then ministered to her. I noticed she had a beautiful face. The realization that I had defeated the biggest and most frightening officer was overwhelming. She said she had never been put down by a recruit before. Prayer was the secret weapon. Then I got up and left and I remember that everyone was watching me with shocked looks upon their faces.

After all, that had never been done before!

I awakened and thought, "What did the dream mean?" Then I began to get clarity.

I believed that God was telling me that there would be a series of hurdles and the last one would be the toughest and defeated *only* by prayer. Only with His help, would I survive and live to defeat the last stronghold. Only then could I tell others. That was the reason for writing this book. We must learn our lessons well and put the experiences as weapons into an arsenal for future use. Still, I kept wondering what the lady represented.

My Interpretation of the Dream

As I contemplated the meaning of my dream, I had to run to a hair appointment at Omar's Salon. While turning the dial of the radio, I came upon one of my favorite preachers. He was teaching from the Old Testament. His subject was from the book of Ecclesiastes and he was agreeing with the depressing sentiment expressed by the author of the book. Then he made this comment,

"As Ecclesiastes says, who is really going to remember you or what you did? Even men like Julius Caesar, Napoleon or George Washington are soon forgotten." That made me angry, after all, the reason we can talk about them, is that they *are* remembered. Also God's Word says in Malachi 3 that the Lord listened and heard and a scroll of remembrance was written in His presence concerning those who feared the Lord. Wasn't His eye on the sparrow? He knows and counts every hair on our head. He recounts every idle word that is said. I Corinthians 8:3 reminds us that the man who loves God, is known by Him. I turned the dial off.

As Mike colored my hair, we discussed the recent chapter in the book of Jonah about the worm. When I mentioned how angry I was at what the preacher said, Mike made the most amazing comment,

"Well, I guess you found *your worm!*"

"Eureka," I shouted. "Preachers unscriptual doctrine are the worms and the beautiful woman in fatigues represented the church. Only massive amounts of prayer would allow you to handle the trials and conflicts of this life and even the 'church worms.' When you wrestle these two, you better dress the part and throw on a pair of fatigues like my girls do when they go to football games.

Not so long ago, Pastor Dotty Schmitt of Immanuel's Church in Maryland wrote a book called, *The Bride Wears Combat Boots,* all I can say to that is Amen. SHE better!

As I went home that day, I was relaying the day's events to my son Pete, an ardent Florida football Gator fan. He shook his head in disbelief at what the preacher said and then made a profound comment about the University of Florida's head football coach,

"Mom, Steve Spurrier would never encourage his football team before a major game, by asking them, after all who really cares or remembers who won the National Championship last year and the year before. Especially not before a major football game, that would discourage the team. How good would they play after a pep talk like that?" He was right. Sometimes, kids have more sense than adults.

The lessons I learned are priceless and so I pass them on that others might benefit. God's plan in the lessons I learned was not only to change me but to have me successfully confront the challenges that beset me, so I might prevail. For the casual observer, my serene countenance might denote apathy or passiveness but in reality nothing could be further from the truth.

By learning to refrain from attacking people and focusing trust on God, we insure that the focus becomes the obstacle that we need to overcome. This is a powerful truth! So many individuals in difficult circumstances end up wounding and spearing comrades in arms. Your family and friends are on your side. Cooperate and allow God to use these tremendous challenges to change you from the inside out. This is the secret to receiving your miracle and overcoming the numerous hurdles that stretch across your path.

Run the Race

Two of my neighbors are runners; Barb Johnson and Karen Ritter. Karen is a long distance runner having competed in numerous races including the prestigious Boston Marathon. What amazed me was her commitment to train. She invested an incredible amount of time, physical strength and expense to run the race. She even hired a trainer so when she competed, she could finish the race and she did.

She ended up doing so well that she was invited to participate again. No one ever competes in a race of this magnitude without realizing that there is a tremendous price to pay for participating successfully. If that is true just imagine what sacrifice it takes to win?

> *Do you not know that those who run in a race all run, but only one receives the prize? Run in such a way that you may win. And everyone who competes in the games exercises self-control in all things. They then do it to receive a perishable wreath, but we an imperishable.*

> I Corinthians 9:24 &25

When you find yourself in a seemingly impossible situation, realize you did not get there overnight. Therefore, it may take as much time to trek out of the woods as it took to get into the woods. Some folks toss up a half hearted prayer and expect God to answer with a lightning bolt and by golly it better be sooner than later. If you expect to win, then put forth the effort and train like my friend Karen.

People often say that God doesn't answer prayer because He didn't swoop down instantly with a fiery chariot and remove them from the problem. When in reality they willfully continued to stay in the mess, refusing to embrace a new direction. They are their own worst enemy. In this case ignorance is not bliss but it is disingenuous and disobedient. Changing poor lifestyle habits may be needed before the race can be won.

I liken it to a certain woman who knew that she needs to do something with her hair. So she went to the store to buy a hairstyle magazine. When she found one she liked, she had to make an appointment with the stylist. The process of change had begun. After Omar gave her a new cut, he showed her some new products and how to fix her hair when she got home. The benefits of a new attractive hair style took time and a commitment to change.

A Spiritual Journey Takes Time

Healing works like that. You must plow the field so God can plant the seeds. I eventually not only received healing but also revelation knowledge about God, more than I could have dreamed possible. Remember to prayerfully approach God honestly with your shortcomings and be patient with yourself. The process will take you on a journey about changing *you*. Be patient and realize that your healing may take time, after all Rome wasn't built in a day. Read the Word and mediate on it continually. Give God time to enlighten the eyes of your understanding. Wisdom and knowledge from God's word will light your path and keeping you from failing. To know God is the most wonderful thing that an individual can experience.

By doggedly enduring, I reached my goal. Oh taste and see that the Lord is good. Trusting Him was my greatest challenge. Even today I have many unanswered questions.

God does answer prayer. By submitting to Him, we give Him honor, the respect He deserves and then the opportunity for Him to act on our behalf.

When you pray, decide to make the same commitment to God that you expect God to make to you.

When you get to an obstacle, pray and then take time to listen. Don't assume and presume on how your prayer will be answered. Humble yourself and let God show you whether or not you need to go over, around, under or even through the obstacle. Pray as if everything depended on Him and act as though everything depended on you.

He has heard and in His perfect time, He will answer you. While you are waiting for God to do the miracle *you do your part.* Get your heart and mind lined up to His way of thinking and acting. Many times God's healing involves changing patterns of thinking. You can get sick again in no time because you're thinking is messed up. I call it "stinking' thinking." "Religious" bad attitudes, unforgiveness, hatred, grudge-keeping, to name a few will keep you just as sick as any of those other more blatant "sins." Often folks wonder why they are still sick when they attend church! As I have said before, just because you sit in a garage doesn't make you a car!

They could be poisoning their own minds and consequently their bodies that God designed to think pure and clean thoughts. Like filling a well full with putrid contents from a cesspool and then wondering why the water is polluted. Eventually the well is rotted by the contents. So it is with the human body that the Creator designed.

The body works best within the confines of the owner's manual, the Bible. In my case there were so many attitudes and ways of thinking that had to be dealt with that it took two long years of constantly studying my Bible and praying (many times all night) to right the wrong. God cannot do the work for you because that involves the will and God will not violate a person's will. The illness exposed and brought to the forefront wrong attitudes and a mindset that were always there. ***Exposing the wrong thinking was His job but changing my mind* was my job,** *agreeing with Him was my job, seeing things the way He sees things was my job.*

So I continually repented and told God I was sorry. That's what forgiveness is, saying you're sorry and meaning it and then actually changing with His help. Sometimes I had a hissy fit first and then said I was sorry. I could picture God patiently waiting until my tantrum was over and then I would say. Agree with what God says about someone not the devil.

"Lord, I know I'm wrong but that person, blah blah blah is so difficult." Then I would say, God, help me to love so and so even though they drive me crazy. When I prepared myself He came and gave me the power and ability to love them.

Where there was hatred or condescension or even irritation, there would be mercy, love and compassion. To explain what it is like to be filled and be a vessel that carries love and the heart of God instead of fear and a bad attitude is the most wonderful thing imaginable. It is like touching the face of God! Changing may appear to be simple but it is certainly not easy. All I know is that I would never in a million years go back to the way I was. I made the commitment and nothing was going to keep me from my miracle *not even me!*

When the lessons were learned, and the testing was over, the actual miracle took almost no time at all. All material was reviewed, I knew deep inside that it was time for the big final exam. When I finally passed the exam, graduation day came and I was ready to receive my diploma. Hallelujah my miracle was in hand!

Like the children of Israel putting their shoes on and packing their bags and preparing the Lord's Passover, the time had come for me to leave Egypt and slavery forever.

> *"Now you shall eat it, in this manner: with your loins girded, your sandals on your feet, and your staff n your hand; and you shall eat it in haste, it is the Lord's Passover." And it came about at the end of four hundred and thirty years, to the very day, which all the hosts of the Lord went out from the land of Egypt.*

Exodus 11:11 &41

Like the children of Israel when time came, nothing could stop them from leaving Egypt.

Finally, beloved, humble yourself and acknowledge that *you* are not God and that you need help from Him and others. His wisdom, His strength, His mercy and His grace will help you to the finish line in victory. Don't let foolish pride and independence rob you of a destiny filled with life, peace and health. Remember too that you may be the miracle in someone else's life.

If it takes baby steps, just keep going until you are walking strong and confident. You are not alone for others are on the side lines cheering you to victory and God is always present within you. It is my prayer that you will be abundantly blessed and that God will use my book to encourage you on your own spiritual journey.

> *I shall live and not die and declare the works of God.*

Psalm 118:17

Chapter Review

1. **Are you willing to make the necessary changes, remove any impediment so the Lord can answer your prayers?**

   _____

   _____

   _____

2. **If the answer to #1 was yes, list any challenging areas of change that come to mind. Now take a moment and prayerfully commit them to the Lord.**

   _____

   _____

   _____

Epilogue & Two Letters

Reflection at the Pool

It had been three months since I had my kidney transplant. This was the first time I had been swimming in quite a while. Usually when I did my laps, I would jump in the water quickly and begin my workout but I couldn't help to just look at the beautiful clear pool water. I was overcome with thankfulness and emotion that God had allowed me to live through such amazing events.

Tears began to roll down my checks, as I realized how blessed I was. Jenny the girl who did pool maintenance came over quickly to make sure I was all right. I assured her I was. Then, she asked me where I had been these many months?

"Jenny it's a long story," I began to briefly recount some of the events that I'd been through as I sat on the side of the pool.

I shared about all the wonderful people that had prayed, inspired and encouraged me with words like my Uncle George's bumper sticker that read, 'Keep on Truckin with Jesus'. I remembered the words that my Mother had written to me in an inspiring letter when all of this had just begun.

October 10, 1996

Dear Eileen,

I want you to do everything within your power to regain your strength. Use everything God has given you both spiritually and mentally... Be a determined person during this adversity that you are facing.

With all my love for your family I remain,

Your loving Mother

P.S. Enclosed is a check to help during these trying times.

Before I knew it, Jenny had tears in her eyes and had given me a big hug,

"Well, I sure am glad you're all right now, Mrs. Austin." Then she added, "I hope your swim is extra special today." I jumped in the cool water and began to do my laps. I thought about all of the events, and decided that one day I would have to write a book about all I'd been through. Hopefully, it would help people like the ones I had met along the way.

I had learned so much through it all. As I was thinking on all these things, someone's words interrupted my thoughts. The words in my mind were so commanding that I stopped swimming and stood up in the pool.

"No, you will write two books."

There was no question about Who that inner voice was. I recognized Him immediately.

The Holy Ghost had spoken to me once again. God had woven every thread of my experiences into a marvelous tapestry of a story that you now hold within your hands.

Dr. Serrano had asked me before my transplant why I would take such a risk now that I was somewhat stable on dialysis. I explained to him that I wanted to be well every day not just every other day. After Kathy Muni's fast, I decided to go on a fast of my own to seek God for more answers. One final evening, as I sat alone and prayed on a grassy hill overlooking the golf course, I was convinced that I needed to proceed with the transplant surgery. God reminded me of an amazing thing. He said it was the strength, that my Mother lived before me all my early childhood days that gave me the courage to go on day after day.

As I looked up into heaven, I reminded Him,

"But Lord, I told everyone that I would never have a transplant." At that point God spoke to my heart again, asking me who was really preventing me from moving forward?

"Pride," I answered.

He seemed to speak again,

"'I have made the provision and it is up to you whether or not to take it."

Many other wonderful and intimate things He spoke to me that day. I cried off and on for a week, realizing the gravity of my decision. The long night of the soul was finally over. Then, I proceeded to make the arrangements for my transplant. After prayer and fasting, I was convinced beyond a shadow of a doubt that this was the provision that God had for me.

As I meditated on the Word of God two solid years, I became so convinced and assured of my healing that when it finally came it was almost anticlimactic. The final pages of this book contain the letters that Rick and I sent out to inform the friends and family members of our decision.

When I was contemplating the transplant surgery in the spring of 1998, I attended a meeting where Pastor Wally Quinn was preaching. After Wally's preaching, he asked me to come forward. He said something that so amazed me because of the unusual way he worded it. He said that the adversity was over and the (evil) assignment that was against me had been broken.

He had used the *exact* same word 'adversity' that my mother had written in the letter two years before. A coincidence? Never! My ears pricked up, God certainly knew how to confirm the message that I had received from Him in prayer. My words in my mother's letter came back to me. I'm convinced that God had used a word that I would quickly recognize as a further sign that it was truly all right for me to proceed and have the surgery.

God wanted me whole. Of that I was convinced. If I must take another leap of faith then so be it. For many months I carried around a paper bookmark that had the following words on it. God may tell you to go forward, even when it looks hopeless because He may have an even greater miracle in mind.

In my case, He surely did.

First Letter

August 14, 1998

Beloved friends and family,

This letter is to inform our friends and loved ones of our plan for Eileen to have a kidney transplant operation. We are asking you to agree in prayer with us for a supernaturally successful surgery and recovery.

Both of Eileen's sisters volunteered to be the donor, but only one is needed. Eileen is to receive a kidney from her sister, Dr. Leilani Doty. We will be in her debt for such a sacrifice. The surgery is scheduled for Friday August 28, 1998. Dr. Victor Bowers is to be the surgeon.

We want to say thank you for all of your prayers, music, tapes, books, calls, letters, and numerous other things that you have done that have supported us over these last two years. We are eager for closure on this chapter, and anticipate a highly successful surgery for both Eileen and Leilani. We have learned many things over the course of this ordeal, and Eileen is thinking of writing about them when this is over.

Because of the nature of transplant surgery, Eileen will have to be isolated for a time following the operation. She will not be allowed to have either visitors or flowers. We are trusting that you will understand this precaution. The most important thing that anyone can do for us is to pray. Please pray according to the following.

THANK GOD FOR:

1)   Guiding Dr. Bower's hands and giving him a supernatural knowledge and understanding and wisdom in the removal of the kidney from Leilani and perfect placement of that kidney into Eileen.

2)   Leilani having a minimum of pain and discomfort. Further that she not experience any disruption to the other organs as the kidney is removed.

3)   The kidney being a perfect match, and further that it begin working immediately upon being implanted. That there be no interference with the existing kidneys as they actually get stronger over the course of time.

4)   A minimum amount of immunity drugs and anti-infection drugs. In fact that the dosages will be reduced so quickly that

no other body parts are injured in any way. No side effects from the drugs, no infections and no other problems. That the reduced need for drugs and medication be so fast that it will amaze the physicians involved.

THANK GOD THAT:

1) Eileen and Leilani will go flying through the procedures and recover in record time.

2) After the surgery there will be no calcium, iron or any other chemical deficiency. All of the body's chemicals will be in proper balance.

That GOD Be Glorified and Honored Through The Whole Procedure

Rick and Eileen Austin

Second Letter

September 13, 1998

Beloved friends and Family,

We want to give everyone an update on Eileen's kidney transplant now that we have some breathing space. As you can imagine it has been quite hectic managing a job, family and taking care of the two recuperating sisters. It has been 2 weeks since the surgery and Eileen and Leilani are doing great. The biggest thing for all of us is to keep them from over doing. We cannot thank each and every one of you enough for the cards, calls, gifts and especially the prayers. The food dishes were especially a blessing as they gave Grace and Rick one less thing to have to do.

The surgery was very successful; and the transplanted kidney began to function as soon as it was connected. That is when Leilani began to refer to it as the "kidney that could", (kind of like The Little Engine that Could) and did in Leilani's words she pictured her kidney looking around and saying, "Well, some body's been slacking off around here and I got a lot of cleaning up to do... better get started." It did!

On Friday afternoon when Dr. Bowers, the surgeon, came out to Rick after the surgery was completed he said everything went as well as could possibly be planned for, hoped for. In other words, everything went great! Although Eileen and Leilani slept a great deal the first few days they were able to get up briefly the very next day. Each subsequent day they got stronger and stronger. It so amazed the doctor's and other hospital staff, that they began to refer to them as the "wonder sisters." On day two after the surgery they were taking short walks. On day three they were walking up and down the hospital corridor. On day four the staff began to remove various apparatus that had been hooked up to Eileen and Leilani ... what a relief and so much easier than having to drag stuff around Eileen asked one of the staff as she removed this big pump, "What is that?" The girl said, "Oh it's the morphine pump, you never used it but you have to pay for it just the same!" The staff was so incredible and went the extra mile, so to speak, in answering our questions and caring for us. We also want to thank the Tampa General Hospital Chaplain, a precious Haitian Pastor, Celillion Alteme. Each day he prayed with the sisters and prior to the surgery he anointed them with oil. He was a great comfort to the sisters.

Eileen jokingly said the staff tried to kick us out on Monday evening but we wouldn't go because the food was too good and we wanted another hospital meal.(just kidding) By Tuesday morning they were being wheeled out of the hospital to continue our recovery at home. Incredible and miraculous is all we can say. They just might become the new poster kids for kidney transplantation.

Especially from Eileen

What was the secret to our incredible experience? Well, we know that you already know. It was the prayers. We are very glad that we sent out that first letter. Thursday evening, before the surgery, my sister and I looked out of the eighth floor window of the hospital we noticed the most magnificent purple sunset over the Tampa Harbor. We said our evening prayers and we felt a serene peace covering us. A fleeting rain shower belted the window and then we saw it... a gorgeous rainbow in the sky, over the harbor, the cruise ships, and us! If I live a gazillion years, (no that isn't a real number, for my elementary readers but you get the idea) I will never be able to explain the peace we experienced during the entire stay. It is truly as the scriptures states, it passes all understanding.

"And the peace of God which passes all comprehension shall guard your hearts and your minds in Christ Jesus. (Philippians 4:7)

At no time did we experience the slightest bit of fear or worry. The prayers of all of you hovered around us. We literally felt their presence and the most wonderful thing of all was to feel the awesome presence of God protecting us. We knew that there would be an unmistakable presence overlooking the entire procedure. Forgive me if I sound preachy but I know God must truly get the credit. We prayed for wisdom and knowledge for the doctors to know exactly the best way to do everything and we were not disappointed. It was truly a miraculous procedure.

Finally, I want to honor my sister, Leilani who willingly and unflinchingly gave her time and countless trips to Tampa and ultimately risked her own life for mine. Jesus said this the night he was betrayed, at the last supper right before He laid down His life for us on the cross, "Greater love has no one than this, that he lay down his life for his friends."(John 15:13) That is exactly what my sister did for me. I was imprisoned and unable to provide a solution to my dilemma but she willingly sacrificed and gave her kidney, her time, her health. I was told that for the donor it is much more painful because of where the surgeons have to go into the back to get the kidney. She did not need the morphine either, and did fantastic throughout the entire procedure. When I was able to walk I kissed her again and again and said thank you for setting me free from my prison. It was also a very emotional time for us as you can imagine. I can not express to you the bond we feel. There are no words that can possibly express the love I have, the honor I feel of knowing her. My admiration for her is very great. She truly is a modem day hero.

I want to add that my other sister Darlene and my mother said they would willingly donate a kidney for me. I am truly blessed. Yesterday I had the opportunity to talk with someone who said his siblings would not do that for him. I am truly blessed and I want to express my heartfelt thanks to my husband and children, Peter, Grace. Joy and Andy, who have stood with me through this difficult ordeal. I never could have done it without them.

Well, the goal was to make this short and sweet and to the point but it's beginning to sound and look like a miniseries. We cannot convey enough our heartfelt thanks to you for your love, and especially the prayers. Whatever else God allows me to accomplish in this life know that you are a part of that because you prayed us through one of the roughest phases of our lives. God bless you richly.

Your loved ones,

Rick and Eileen Austin

Pete, Grace, Joy and Andy

Bibliography

Anderson, Understanding the Old Testament (Englewood Cliffs, N.J.: Prentice-Hall, Inc. 1957) pp.192, 202, 204-206, 218, 212-213.

Bragg, Patricia, The Miracle of Fasting (Santa Barbara, CA: Health Science 1998).

Elijah, The New American Desk Encyclopedia (New York: Concord Reference Book 1989), p. 407.

Jones Doug, What You must Understand (Tulsa, Oklahoma: Rhema Healing Tapes Series 1996).

Malcom, Howard, Bible Dictionary (Boston: Dewolf, Fiske &Co.1859), p.209.

Marshall, Katherine, A Man Called Peter (New York: McGraw Hill & Co.1951).

Morison, Samuel, Christopher Columbus, *Mariner* (New York: Little Brown & co. 1955), pp.44-57.

Osborn, T.L., Healing the Sick, (Tulsa, Oklahoma: Harrison House 1977).

Packer, Tenney, White Jr., Land of the Bible (Nashville: Thomas Nelson Publishers 1985), pp. 18, 39, 114.

Prince, Derek, Shaping History Through Prayer and Fasting (Old Tappen, NJ: Fleming H. Revell Company 1973), p.77- 80.

Ten Boom, Corrie, The Hiding Place (Uhrichsville, Ohio: Barbour Publ. Inc.1971) p.211.

Wetheral, Johnson, The Minor Prophets The Books of Elijah & Jonah (Bible Study Fellowship 1962) pp. 1-10.

Unger, Merrill F., Unger's Bible Dictionary (Chicago: Moody Press 1966), p.796.